The George Catlin Book
of American Indians

The George Catlin Book of American Indians

by Royal B. Hassrick

PROMONTORY PRESS

First published in 1977 in New York by Watson-Guptill Publications, a division of Billboard Publications, Inc.,
1515 Broadway, New York, NY 10036

This edition published in the United States of America in 1981 by
Promontory Press
95 Madison Avenue
New York, New York 10016
By arrangement with Watson-Guptill Publications

Library of Congress Catalog Card Number: 81-81163
ISBN: 0-88394-046-9
Printed in the United States of America

CONTENTS

COLOR PLATES

BLACK AND WHITE PLATES

CHRONOLOGY

1796 Born in Wilkes-Barre, Pennsylvania. Son of Putnam Catlin and Sally Sutton.

1817 Read law in Litchfield, Connecticut under Judge Tapping Reeves and James Gould.

1818 Passed bar examination and began practicing law in Lucerne, Pennsylvania.

1820 Set up studio on Walnut Street, Philadelphia.

1822 Exhibited miniatures at the Pennsylvania Academy, Philadelphia.

1824 Elected Academician of the Pennsylvania Academy of Fine Arts, Philadelphia.

1826 Painted portrait of Red Jacket, the Seneca Sachem, at Buffalo, New York.

1828 Exhibited twelve paintings at the American Academy of Fine Arts.

1829 Painted Iroquois Indians in New York State, also Ottowas and Mohegans.

1830 Sojourned to St. Louis. Accompanied William Clark to paint Omahas, Sioux, Missouris, Iowas, and Sac and Foxes. Later, at Leavenworth, he painted Eastern Indians removed to the West—Shawnees, Delawares, Peorias, Potawatomis, Weas, Kaskaskias and Kickapoos as well as Iowas from the West. In the late fall he painted Kansas Indians in their villages on the Kansas River.

1831 Painted Pawnees, Otos, Missouris, and Omahas.

1832 Left St. Louis for the upper Missouri. Painted Blackfeet, Crows, Mandans, and Hidatsas. Also painted Black Hawk at Jefferson Barracks near St. Louis.

1834 Painted Comanches, Kiowas, and Wichitas.

1835 Painted Ojibwas and Sac and Foxes.

1836 Visited Pipestone Quarry. Painted Ojibwas, Winnebagos and Menomonees.

1837 Exhibited his "Gallery" at Clinton Hall, New York.

1838 Held exhibition at the Old Theatre, Washington, D.C.

1839 Exhibited his "Gallery" in London.

1841 Published *Letters and Notes on the Manners, Customs and Conditions of the North American Indians*. 2 Volumes (London).

1844 Published *North American Indian Portfolio,* London.

1845 Exhibited his "Gallery" at the Louvre, Paris.

1848 Returned with his "Gallery" to London.

1853 Made expedition to South America.

1856 Another expedition to Tierra del Fuego, Panama, and later to the Northwest Coast.

1861 Published *Life Amongst the Indians* (Sampson Low).

1867 Published *O-Kee-Pa,* London.

1868 Brussels painting Cartoon collection.

1871 Exhibition of Cartoons in New York City.

1872 Exhibition at Smithsonian Institution, Washington, D.C. Lived in Turret Room at the Smithsonian. Died on December 23 in Jersey City, New Jersey.

PREFACE

While there are many books about Catlin, as well as sections in books which include illustrations of his works, none has devoted attention exclusively to his "Indian Gallery." Now in the National Collection of Fine Arts, Washington, D.C., the works included in this book were chosen to show the scope of Catlin's style and subject matter, and also to include representative individuals from each of the tribes he visited. The illustrations are placed in a sequence based upon the culture areas to which each tribe belonged, beginning with the Indians of the Southeastern Woodlands and moving north to the Great Lakes and the Midwest, and finally to the Great Plains.

The many quotations from Catlin's writings are included not only to interpret what the artist saw and painted, but also in the hope that his words will bring to the reader something of the vitality he expressed in his marvelous "Indian Gallery."

I am especially indebted to the staff of the National Collection of Fine Arts for making this book a reality. To Dr. Joshua C. Taylor, Director, whose encouragement was instrumental in its inception; to Harry Jordan, Administrator, for making the arrangements between the publisher and the National Collection of Fine Arts; and to William Truettner, Curator of Eighteenth and Nineteenth Century Painting and Sculpture, for his generous assistance and enthusiastic help in checking dates, I am most grateful. To the Registrar of the National Collection of Fine Arts, Robert Johnston, for his most efficient system and able assistance, and to Joanna Pessa of the Office of the Registrar for her untiring and cooperative help in selecting photographs, I give my sincere thanks. I am also grateful to Russell Bourne, Editor of Special Publications, for his cooperation.

I am indebted to Donald Holden, Editorial Director of Watson-Guptill, for his unfailing encouragement and strong support of this project, and to my wife, Barbara, who cheerfully and most quickly edited and typed the manuscript.

Royal B. Hassrick

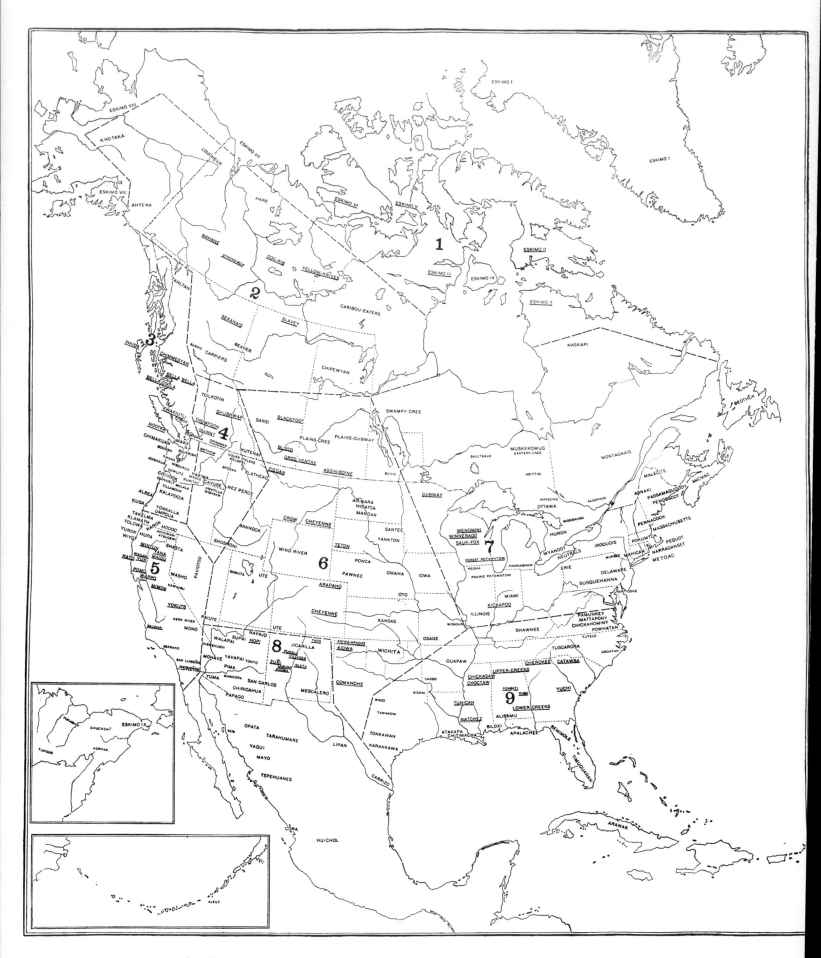

ESKIMO I

ESKIMO VIII

KHOTANÁ

ESKIMO VII

ESKIMO VII:

LOUCHEUX

ESKIMO VII

ESKIMO VI

ESKIMO V

ESKIMO II

ESKIMO I

AHTENA

1

ESKIMO III

ESKIMO IV

NAHANE

HARE

ESKIMO II

STRONG-BOW

DOG-RIB

YELLOW-KNIVES

TAHLTAN

2

CARIBOU-EATERS

NASKAPI

SEKANAIS

SLAVEY

HAIDA

CHIMMESYAN

BABINE

CARRIERS

BEAVER

CHIPEWYAN

BEOTHUK

3

BELLA BELLA

TCILKOTIN

SWAMPY-CREE

WAKIUTLI

SHUSWAP

SARSI

BLACKFOOT

PLAINS-OJIBWAY

MONTAGNAIS

NOOTKA

THOMPSON

LILLOET

4

KUTENAI

BLOOD

GROS VENTRE

SWAMPY-CREE

MALECITE

CHIMAKUAN

MAKA

CHILCAGAN

COEUR D'ALENE

KALISPEL

PIEGAN

ASSINIBOINE

SAULTEAUX

MUSKEKOWUG
EASTERN CREE

MICMAC

PASSAMAQUODDY

BORDEN

SQUAMISH

SPOKAN

BUNGI

ABITTIBI

ABNAKI

PENOBSCOT

TWANA

YAKIMA

FLATHEAD

CHENALI

NIBUUALLI

MOLALA

CAYUSE

UMATILLA

NEZ PERCE

NIPISSING

PENNACOOK

DOWLITZ

KLIKITAT

ALGONKIN

CHINDOK

TILLAMOOK

OTTAWA

MASSACHUBETTS

ALBEA

KALAPOOIA

ARIKARA
HIDATSA
MANDAN

OJIBWAY

HURON

POKUMTUK

KUSA

YONKALLA
UMPQUA

SANTEE

MENOMINI
WINNEBAGO
SAUK-FOX

7

WYANDOT

NEUTRALS

IROQUOIS

MAHICAN

PEQUOT

TAKELMA

KAROK

MODOC

CROW

CHEYENNE

YANKTON

MUNSEE

NARRAGANSET

KLAMATH

ACHOMAWI

BANNOCK

FOREST POTAWATOMI

ERIE

METOAC

YUROK

HUPA

ATSUGEWI

TETON

PIANKASHAW

DELAWARE

WIYOT

WINTUN

SHASTA

WIND RIVER

PONCA

PRAIRIE POTAWATOMI

PEORIA

SUSQUEHANNA

TANA

MAIDU

SHOSHONI

OMAHA

IOWA

MIAMI

KATO

YUKI

WASHO

6

PAWNEE

OTO

KICKAPOO

POMO

WAPPO

5

PAVIOTSO

GOSIUTE

UTE

ARAPAHO

MISSOURI

ILLINOIS

PAMUNKEY
MATTAPONY
CHICKAHOMINY
POWHATAN

MIWOK

KAWAISU

KANSAS

OSAGE

SHAWNEE

TUTELO

YOKUTS

CHEYENNE

YOKUTS

KERN RIVER

PAIUTE

MONO

MALIBAN

SERRANO

PUEBLO

UTE

NAVAJO

SUPAI

HOPI

TAOS

JICARILLA

KIOWA-APACHE

KIOWA

WICHITA

CADDO

QUAPAW

TUSCARORA

CROATAN

CHEROKEE

CATAWBA

SAN LUISENO

MOHAVE

YAVAPAI

TONTO

8

ZUNI

KERES

ISLETA

COMANCHE

UPPER-CREEKS

DIEGUENO

PIMA

SAN CARLOS

CHICKASAW

CHOCTAW

KOASATI

YUCHI

YUMA

MARICOPA

CHIRICAHUA

MESCALERO

WADO

NICHAI

KUSO

LOWER-CREEKS

PAPAGO

TAWAKONI

TUNICAN

ALIBAMU

OPATA

TARAHUMARE

AENI

LIPAN

TONKAWAN

KARANKAWA

NATCHEZ

BILOXI

ATAKAPA
CHITIMACHA

APALACHEE

SEMINOLE

YAQUI

MAYO

CARRIZO

TIMUQUANAN

9

TEPEHUANES

CORA

HUICHOL

ARAWAK

TURAUSK

CHUCKCHI

ESKIMO IX

TUNGUS

KORYAK

ALEUT

Cultural Area Map of North America as of 1650 showing location of Indian tribes. Areas identified by number: 1. Eskimo, 2. Mackenzie, 3. Northwest Coast, 4. Plateau, 5. California, 6. Plains, 7. Northeast Woodlands, 8. Southwest, 9. Southeast Woodlands.

INTRODUCTION

George Catlin's "Indian Gallery" was an amazing accomplishment. And so was George Catlin an amazing man. Painter, author, ethnographer, historian, traveler, and showman, he was indeed a versatile character. Moreover, he was determined, courageous and, for his time, compassionately farsighted in his appreciation of Indians and their culture. He brought knowledge, entertainment, understanding, and beauty to thousands.

Early Years

Born on July 26, 1796 in Wilkes-Barre, Pennsylvania, Catlin grew up with a love of fishing and hunting and not much attachment to his school books.

He preferred hunting for arrowheads and Indian relics and, as Catlin put it, "occasional dabblings with the brush, which had secured already a corner in my affections." Sixteen years before Catlin was born, his mother had been captured by Indians during the Wyoming massacre of 1778, and Catlin loved to hear the stories of the Indian frontier. However, his father, an attorney, persuaded Catlin to enter the field of law. This he did, reading for two years under the supervision of Reeve and Gould in Litchfield, Connecticut. Upon admission to the bar, he set up practice in Lucerne, Pennsylvania. Two or three years were enough. He sold his law books, bought brushes and paint pots with the proceeds, moved to Philadelphia, and set out to be a painter.

Without a teacher or even an advisor, this self-taught man had fair success as a painter of portraits, especially miniatures. Moving in the circle of such recognized artists as Charles Willson Peale, Rembrandt Peale, and Thomas Sully, he was surely influenced by them, particularly by Sully. Catlin was an able enough painter to be elected to the prestigious Pennsylvania Academy of the Fine Arts in 1824. Four years later, he exhibited twelve of his paintings at the American Academy of Fine Arts. Catlin had arrived.

But Catlin was restless, as he says, "continually reaching for some branch or enterprise of the art, on which to devote a whole lifetime of enthusiasm." It took a delegation of Indians, passing through Philadelphia to Washington, to crystallize his musings. Ten or fifteen Indians from the Far West, proud and stoic, arrayed in their dramatic costumes and plumed bonnets, and carrying shields, paraded around the city to the astonishment and admiration of everyone. Catlin was entranced. When they departed, Catlin was left with a heartfelt regret. After long and deep pondering, he had an inspiration, an idea to which he could dedicate his life and fulfill his goals.

"Black and blue cloth and civilization are destined, not only to veil, but to obliterate the grace and beauty of Nature. Man, in the simplicity and loftiness of his nature, unrestrained and unfettered by the disguises of art, is surely the most beautiful model for the painter — and the country from which he hails is unquestionably the best study or school of the arts in the world: such I am sure, from the models I have seen, is the wilderness of North America. And the history and customs of such a people, preserved by pictorial illustrations, are themes worthy of the lifetime of one man, and nothing short of the loss of my life, shall prevent me from visiting their country, and becoming their historian."[1]

Now Catlin had a project, but he had more than that. Without quite realizing it, by planning a pictorial record of the American Indians, he was preparing a taxonomic classification, much as John James Audubon was doing for American bird life, in the truly scientific vogue of the day. Moreover, by becoming the Indians' historian — he later published his *Letters and Notes on the Manners, Customs and Condition of the North American Indians* (two volumes, London, 1841) — Catlin was one of the nation's pioneer anthropologists. If Lewis Henry Morgan's study of the Iroquois' social system was original, so, in its way, was Catlin's ethno-historical approach.

It is interesting to note that Catlin had painted Indian portraits before his definite decision to make this his life's work. In 1826, he did a portrait of the famed Seneca orator, Red Jacket, and three years later, while again visiting western New York, painted several Iroquois, as well as Mohegans and an Ottawa Indian. Catlin must have made notes about this trip, for his observations and comments appear in his "Letter 47." Here he indulged Red Jacket by posing him "that he might be seen on the Table Rock and the Falls of Niagra, about which place he thought his spirit would linger after he was dead." Nonetheless, Catlin's idea at this time was not crystallized, for he was still based in the East.

Catlin's plans were met with skepticism. When he informed his friends, they outlined every obstacle and every danger, rather than support him. His plans found favor with no one, and he broke with them all, even with his wife and aged parents. As it turned out, he was "his only advisor and protector."

The Far West

Catlin was not easily discouraged. Undaunted and in high spirits he left civilization for what was then the "Far West" in 1830. Equipped with paints, palette, canvas, and easel, he "set out on my arduous and perilous undertaking with the determination of reaching ultimately, every tribe of Indians on the Continent of North America, and of bringing home faithful portraits of their principal personages, both men and women, from each tribe, views of their villages, games, etc., and full notes on their character and history. I designed, also, to procure their costumes, and a complete collection of their manufactures and weapons, and to perpetuate them in a *Gallery unique,* for the use and instruction of future ages."[2] He had a dream, and he felt driven by time. The fast-vanishing races of native men must be recorded and rescued from oblivion.

Reaching St. Louis on the Missouri River, he sought the aid of William Clark of the famed Lewis and Clark expedition, now Superintendent of Indian Affairs. Clark not only was helpful, but he also invited Catlin to accompany him to Fort Crawford at Prairie du Chien. Treaties were being held with various tribes — the Sioux, Missouri, Omaha, Iowa, and the allied Sac and Fox. Here was a golden chance for Catlin to capture portraits.

Catlin gives an interesting description of the Treaty with the allied Sac and Fox. Following the bloody and divisive Black Hawk War of 1812, in which Black Hawk and his followers were defeated, the United States recognized Keokuk as the Head Chief in recognition of his having held two-thirds of the warriors in restraint.

"The Treaty, itself, in all its forms, was a scene of interest, and *Kee-O-kuk* was the principal speaker on the occasion, being recognized as the head-chief of the tribe. He was a very subtle and dignified man, and well fitted to wield the destinies of his nation. The poor, dethroned monarch, old Black Hawk, was present and looked an object of pity. With an old frock coat and brown hat on, and a cane in his hand, he stood the whole time outside of the group, and in dumb and dismal silence, with his sons by the side of him, and also his *quondam* aide-de-camp, Nah-pope, and the prophet."[3]

In the fall of 1830, Catlin painted Northeastern woodland Indians who had been removed by the government to what is now Kansas. Here, near Fort Leavenworth, he found, among others, Shawnees, Delawares, Kickapoos, and Potawatomis. His lament for those displaced tribes—and their despair at the loss of their way of life—is well expressed in his observations about the Kickapoos.

"At present but a small tribe, numbering 600 or 800, the remnant of a once numerous and warlike tribe. They are residing within the State of Illinois, near the south end of Lake Michigan, and living in a poor and miserable condition, although they have one of the finest countries in the world. They have been reduced in numbers by whiskey and smallpox, and the game being destroyed in the country, and having little industry to work, they are exceedingly poor and dependent. In fact, there is very little inducement for them to build houses and cultivate their farms, for they own so large and so fine a tract of country, which is now completely surrounded by civilized settlements, they know, from experience, they will soon be obligated to sell out their country for a trifle, and move to the west. This system of moving has already commenced with them, and a considerable party have located on a tract of lands offered to them on the west bank of the Missouri River, a little north of Fort Leavenworth."[4]

Later that same year, Clark visited the Kansas Indians and Catlin may have gone along. Of this tribe, Catlin wrote: "The Konzas, of 1560 souls, reside at the distance of sixty or eighty miles from this place, on the Konzas River, fifty miles above its union with the Missouri, from the West.

"This tribe has undoubtedly sprung from the Osages, as their personal appearance, language and traditions clearly prove. They are living adjoining to the Osages at this time, and although a kindred people, have sometimes deadly warfare with them. The present chief of this tribe is known by the name of the 'White Plume'; a very urbane and hospitable man, of good portly size, speaking some English, and making himself good company for all white persons who travel through his country and have the good luck to shake his liberal and hospitable hand."[5] Catlin was greatly disappointed not to have got this man's portrait.

Also at Leavenworth Catlin painted representatives of Missouri and Platte River tribes: Otoes, Missouris, Omahas, and Pawnees. It would appear that Catlin visited these groups before the smallpox epidemic of 1832, but must have completed his notes at a later date. His writings suggest that he was among them after the scourge. Of the Pawnees, Catlin relates: "The Pawnees are a very powerful and warlike nation, living on the river Platte, about one hundred miles from its junction with the Missouri; laying claim to, and exercising sway over, the whole country, from its mouth to the base of the Rocky Mountains.

"The present number of this tribe is ten or twelve thousand; about one half the number they had in 1832, when that most appalling disease, the small-pox, was accidently introduced amongst them by the Fur Traders, and whiskey sellers; when ten thousand (or more) of them perished in the course of a few months.

"The destructive ravages of this most fatal disease amongst these poor people, who know of no specific for it, is beyond the knowledge, and almost beyond the belief, of the civilized world. Terror and dismay are carried with it; and awful despair, in the midst of which they plunge into the river, when in the highest state of fever, and die in a moment; or dash themselves from precipices; or plunge their knives to their hearts, to rid themselves of the pangs of slow and disgusting death."[6]

Sometime in 1831, while in St. Louis, a group of four Indians appeared as delegates. Representatives of the Plains Cree, Plains

Ojibwa, and Yanktonais Sioux arrived. Catlin missed no opportunities. He painted them.

The Noble Savage

The year 1832, however, brought Catlin the grand opportunity. In the spring he arranged a trip aboard the steamboat *Yellowstone* to ply the Missouri to the American Fur Company's Fort Union, 2,000 miles up the great river to the mouth of the Yellowstone River. Stopping at Fort Pierre, in what is now South Dakota, he painted Teton Sioux Indians and two visiting Cheyennes. At this time, he may also have got the portrait of a Nez Percé and a Flathead dressed in Sioux costumes upon their return from St. Louis, the remnants of a larger group of Plateau Indians who were seeking the truth of the claims made by missionaries.

Farther up the river, Catlin sketched the Arikara villages from the steamboat. Because of past injustices, this tribe was too antagonistic toward the white traders for anyone to dare visit them.

Upon reaching Fort Union, Catlin reveled in what he beheld: the "Noble Savage," unspoiled in his native haunts.

"The several tribes of Indian inhabiting the regions of the Upper Missouri, and of whom I spoke in my last letter, are undoubtedly the finest looking, best equipped, and most beautifully costumed of any on the continent. They live in a country well stocked with buffaloes and wild horses, which furnish them an excellent and easy living; their atmosphere is pure, which produces good health and long life; and they are the most independent and the happiest races of Indians I have met with: they are all entirely in the state of primitive wildness, and consequently are picturesque and handsome, almost beyond description. Nothing in the world, of its kind, can possibly surpass in beauty and grace, some of their games and amusements — their gambols and parades, of which I shall speak and paint hereafter."[7]

It was in this setting that Catlin painted Blackfeet and Crow Indians, among his most inspired works. Leaving the fort in a heavy and awkward "canoe of green timber," accompanied by two traders, Catlin floated down the river to reach the Mandan villages near Fort Clark in what is now North Dakota. Here he not only painted portraits, but remarkable scenes of ceremonies and village life. Catlin spent quite some time, about two weeks, among the Mandans and was deeply impressed.

"They have two villages only, which are about two miles distant from each other; and number in all (as near as I can learn), about 2000 souls. Their present villages are beautifully located, and judiciously also, for defence against the assaults of their enemies. The site of the lower (or principal) town, in particular is one of the most beautiful and pleasing that can be seen in the world, and even more beautiful than imagination could ever create. In the very midst of an extensive valley (embraced with a thousand graceful swells and parapets or mounds of interminable green, changing to blue, as they vanish in distance) is built the city, or principal town of the Mandans. On an extensive plain (which is covered with a green turf, as well as hills and dales, as far as the eye can possibly range, without tree or bush to be seen) are to be seen rising from the ground, and towards the heavens, domes — (not of gold, but) of dirt — and the thousand spears (not spires) and scalp-poles, etc., etc., of the semi-subterraneous village of the hospitable and gentlemanly Mandans."[8]

The following year was spent completing his sketches; not until 1834 did Catlin venture to the field again. From Fort Gibson, Arkansas, he may have traveled to the Osage villages, but more likely he captured likenesses of tribesmen visiting the Fort, since the nearest of their three towns was forty miles away.

"Their present residence is about 700 miles West of the Mississippi River; in three villages, constituted of wigwams, built of barks and flags or reeds.

"The Osages may justly be said to be the tallest race of men in North America, either of red or white skins; there being very few indeed of the men, at their full growth, who are less than six feet in stature, and very many of them six and a half, and others seven feet. They are at the same time well-proportioned in their limbs and good-looking; being rather narrow in the shoulders, and, like most all very tall people, a little inclined to stoop, not throwing the chest out, and the head and shoulders back, quite as much as the Crows and Mandans, and other tribes amongst which I have been familiar. Their movement is graceful and quick; and in war and the chase, I think they are equal to any of the tribes about them."[9]

A Military Expedition

Catlin's major field trip of the year, however, was to accompany the United States Dragoons, under the command of Colonel Henry Dodge, on an expeditionary foray up the Arkansas and Red Rivers. This was the region of the Kiowas, Comanches, and Wichitas. Catlin was thrilled and wrote rather poetically about his impressions.

"Under the protection of the United States' dragoons, I arrived at this place three days since, on my way again in search of the 'Far West.' How far I may *this time* follow the flying phantom, is uncertain. I am already again in the land of the *buffaloes* and the *fleet-bounding antelopes*; and I anticipate with many other beating hearts, rare sport and amusement amongst the wild herds ere long.

"A great part of the way, the country is prairie, gracefully undulating — well watered, and continually beautified by copses and patches of timber. On our way my attention was riveted to the tops of some of the prairie bluffs, whose summits I approached with inexpressible delight. I rode to the top of one of these noble mounds, in company with my friends Lieut. Wheelock and Joseph Chadwick, where we agreed that our *horses* instinctively *looked* and *admired.* They thought not of

the rich herbage that was under their feet, but, with deep-drawn sighs, their necks were loftily curved, and their eyes widely stretched over the landscape that was beneath us. From this elevated spot, the horizon was bounded all around us by mountain streaks of blue, softening into azure as they vanished, the pictured vales that intermediate lay, were deepening into green as the eye was returning from its roamings. Beneath us, and winding through the waving landscape was seen with peculiar effect, the 'bold dragoons', marching in beautiful order, forming a train of a mile in length. Baggage wagons and Indians (*engagés*) helped to lengthen the procession. From the point where we stood, the line was seen in miniature; and the undulating hills over which it was bending its way, give it the appearance of a huge black snake, gracefully gliding over a rich carpet of green."[10]

Upon arriving at the Comanche Village, Catlin collected many portraits, together with scenes of camp life and horsemanship. While the trip was successful as a military show of force and eventually led to peace treaties, the expedition was marred by deathly fever, killing about 150 of the dragoons. Catlin himself suffered miserably and spent much time recuperating upon his return to Fort Gibson.

It was here that Catlin was able to paint Choctaw portraits, as well as the action of a Choctaw ball game. Cherokees and Creeks were also in the vicinity, and he added their portraits to his gallery.

The following year, 1835, Catlin went north to the Falls of Saint Anthony on the Mississippi and then traveled south to Fort Snelling. During this sojourn, he painted Ojibwa and Santee Sioux portraits.

Completing the Indian Gallery

In 1836, Catlin visited the famed Pipestone Quarry in what is now Minnesota. Here the Indians mined the red stone from which they fashioned their sacred pipes. Catlin's visit was not without some difficulty.

He and his English companion, Mr. Robert Serril Wood, were held virtual prisoners by some twenty Sioux Indians who refused to let them trespass on this sacred place. They were subjected to threatening harangues by each of the Indians for an entire afternoon. And when they finished, Catlin and Wood, with more courage than wisdom, mounted their horses and rode off toward the quarry.

Catlin was greatly impressed by the beauty of the red stone quarry and the many Indian legends associated with it. Formerly, tribesmen from many nations "have hidden the war club as they approached it, and stayed the cruelties of the scalping-knife, under the fear of vengeance of the Great Spirit, who overlooks it."

One of the myths describes a great flood. Thousands of Indians sought refuge on the heights of the quarry, but the waters rose and drowned them. The rocks of the quarry were stained red from the flesh of the bodies. And because of this, it became a holy place for all nations. But sometime in the early nineteenth century, the Sioux seized the mine, once open to all, and claimed it as their own.

Catlin collected samples of the stone and sent them to one of the leading mineralogists in the country, Dr. Charles Jackson of Boston. He pronounced it a "new mineral compound" and named it *catlinite* in honor of the artist. When first mined, catlinite is soft and easily carved. When exposed to the air, it soon hardens. On this sojourn, Catlin collected more portraits, including likenesses of Winnebagos and Menominees.

The following year, 1837, Catlin traveled south to Fort Moultrie at Charleston, South Carolina. Here were imprisoned Seminole Indians captured in the long and costly Seminole War. Catlin painted several portraits, including that of the famous Osceola. The painting turned out to be one of Catlin's finest studio portraits. The broken-hearted Osceola died shortly after this painting was completed and was buried at the fort.

By 1837, Catlin had just about completed his "Indian Gallery," some 507 portraits, genre paintings, and landscapes, all of which he listed in his 1840 catalog. He numbered each portrait so that when two or more sitters appeared in a painting, each one received a number. There were actually 422 paintings.

Catlin's Art

As an artist, Catlin was essentially a documentary painter, concerned with facts rather than esthetics. While he had a sense of the sublime and tried to impart it in his landscapes, perspective eluded him, his flat use of color is unimpressive, and his scenes miss the feeling of grandeur. As a portrait painter, however, he was at his best.

Catlin was best at portraying the face. With sparingly smooth brushwork, he not only caught and modeled the facial characteristics of his subjects, but conveyed their pride and dignity. Consequently, his Indians became real people, recognizable as individuals, rather than the stock characters so common in paintings of "the red man."

But even his portraits are often erratic in quality. This inconsistency was largely due to the speed with which he had to work. On his trip to the upper Missouri in 1832, he completed 135 pictures, an average of nearly two a day — and there were many days when he was on shipboard, unable to paint. His time to paint was nearly always limited. Many of his portraits are sketches, some probably dashed off in a matter of minutes.

Luckily, as one wag put it, Catlin was the fastest brush in the West. His mastery of the quick impression saved him and brought his portraits to life. Although Sully's portraits have more "shimmer" in the flesh tones, some of Catlin's faces have quite a Sully-like feeling. Moreover, he captured the racial character of his Indian subjects, a feat few artists, before or since, have achieved so consistently. Working under pressure, Catlin was able to catch a vivid likeness. Many years later, Dr. Washington

Mathews of the Smithsonian Institution took Catlin's two volumes of *Letters*, containing colored line engravings, and showed them to descendants of some of Catlin's subjects, who readily recognized their relatives.

His finest works are his three-quarter figures. His full-length portraits, both standing and sitting, are often out of drawing. Sometimes the head is too large, sometimes too small. The hands are often grotesquely large, and he frequently had trouble with the arms and shoulders. Many of his figures are mere sketches, with attention given to the head alone. Undoubtedly, he was pressed for time, starting a picture in the field and possibly intending to complete the rough draft at a later date. He did work over many of his paintings, finishing them in his studio. But perhaps he never had time to finish them all—or possibly never intended to rework each one. He was certainly not reluctant to place the "unfinished" pictures in his catalog nor to exhibit them. He did, however, once write an apology to the effect that what some of his works might lack in artistic merit, they gained in historic value.

Catlin's art does transcend the technical and esthetic limitations of the artist. His landscapes are flat and skyless, but they do convey the vastness of the Western scene. His genre pictures are slapdash, but they are filled with vigor, spontaneity, and drama. His portraits often seem to be mere field sketches, but the faces are well modeled and convincing; they bring to life unknown people who become real persons forever.

Factual Detail

C atlin's attention to detail was also sporadic. Too often, Catlin hastily hinted at detail. At times, however, he was fairly meticulous, delineating beads, necklaces, ear ornaments, and decorations on clothing and headdresses with care and precision. The designs in the porcupine quills which embellished so many of the costumes, the pictographic painting on men's shirts and robes, as well as the geometric painting found on robes worn by women, were sometimes methodically rendered. Unfortunately some of his renderings of these designs were quite inaccurate.

His full-length portrait of the Mandan Mah-To-Toh-Pa (or Four Bears) is a good example of his attention to detail. It has been noted that Catlin may have exaggerated the length of the shirt. Now in the collection of the United States National Museum in Washington, D.C., the actual garment is considerably shorter than Catlin rendered it. But the Swiss artist, Karl Bodmer, painted Four Bears a year later, wearing a similar shirt of almost identical length as that Catlin painted. It is entirely possible that the shirt simply shrank. The collections had suffered two fires and water damage.

In his paintings of costumes, Catlin was faithful in his reproduction of color. The native Americans were limited in their use of colors to red ochre, charcoal black, and occasionally chalk white. When trade goods were introduced—bright textiles and glassy beads—the Indians were quick to attire themselves in these gaudy novelties. Catlin's ability to convey the colorful panoply is seen in his paintings of the Eastern Indians, who had already received such manufactured articles. Catlin's eye for color was sound: his rendering of flesh tones and the muted tans of tanned animal skins was correct.

Catlin's scenes of village life, dances, and buffalo hunts are indeed hasty sketches—and sometimes muddy ones. In his eagerness to convey the action, the spirit, and the feeling—in which he was entirely successful—he sacrificed precision. In his drawings of villages, his tipis appear as flat triangles, each the same size; the fact is that tipis varied, depending upon the wealth and status of the occupants. His earth lodges are rendered as mere domes, without the usual covered entryway, and they, too, were actually of different sizes.

Drawn in the style that was popular in his day, Catlin's horses are academic: they appear to be more Arabian in head and conformation than the mustangs really were. Buffaloes have caused trouble for many artists, and Catlin had his share of difficulties. While he captured the action and conveyed the brute size of these animals, some are more hogshaped than bison-like. His wolves, too, are queer little creatures, but they *are* vicious.

Art critics are not the only authorities who have complained about Catlin's work. Anthropologists have levied charges of inaccuracy against him. Comparing his work with that of Karl Bodmer, they find Catlin's lack of attention to detail disappointing. Bodmer was a young Swiss artist who accompanied Maximilian, Prince of Wied, on a scientific expedition to the Upper Missouri in 1833. Academically trained in the European tradition, his watercolors (and later hand-colored engravings) are masterpieces of detail. Covering the same territory — and in fact painting some of the same subjects as Catlin did the previous year — Bodmer's works are an ethnologist's dream come true. Minute elements of costume are portrayed with photographic clarity. Beads can be counted; design elements and porcupine quill work can be closely studied. His figures are never out of drawing, and his portraits are proud and stoic. On the other hand, too many of Bodmer's figures appear as lifeless as dummies in a wax museum. His Indians are caricatures of what he *thought* he was seeing — fierce, savage redskins. He never had Catlin's empathic ability to capture the Indians' very human qualities. Bodmer's Indians match the stereotype of the period; Catlin's are the genuine article, the real Indians.

In most instances, Catlin's subjects were chosen for him. The leading men were insistent that it was their prerogative to be painted first, and this left the artist little choice. Catlin has written some amusing and illuminating observations about this.

"Whilst painting the portraits of the chiefs and braves of the Sioux, as described in my last epistle, my painting room was the continual rendezvous of the worthies of the tribe; and I, the 'lion of the day', and my art, the *summum* and *ne plus ultra* of mysteries, which engaged the whole conversation of chiefs and sachems, as well as of women and children. I mentioned that I have been obliged to paint them according to rank, as they looked upon the operation as a very great honour, which I, as 'a great chief and medicine-man' was conferring on all who sat to me. Fortunate it was for me, however, that the honour was not a sufficient inducement for all to overcome their fears, which often stood in the way of their consenting to be painted; for if all had been willing to undergo the operation, I should have progressed but a very little way in the *'rank and file'* of their worthies; and should have had to leave many discontented, and (as they would think) neglected. About one in five or eight was willing to be painted, and the rest thought they would be much more sure of 'sleeping quiet in their graves' after they were dead, if their pictures were not made. By this lucky difficulty I got great relief, and easily got through with those who were willing, and at the same time decided by the chiefs to be worthy, of so signal an honour.

"After I had done with the chiefs and braves, and proposed to paint a few of the women, I at once got myself into a serious perplexity, being heartily laughed at by the whole tribe, both by men and women, for my exceeding and (to them) unaccountable condescension in seriously proposing to paint a woman; conferring on her the same honour that I had on the chiefs and braves . . .

"The first reply that I received from those whom I had painted, was, that if I was to paint women and children, the sooner I destroyed *their* pictures, the better; for I had represented to them that I wanted their pictures to exhibit to white chiefs, to show who were the most distinguished and worthy of the Sioux; and their women had never taken scalps, nor did anything better than make fires and dress skins. I was quite awkward in this dilemma in explaining to them that I wanted the portraits of the women to hang *under* those of their husbands, merely to show how their women *looked,* and how they *dressed,* without saying any more of them. After some considerable delay of my operations, and much deliberation on the subject, through the village, I succeeded in getting a number of women's portraits . . . ."[11]

The Indian Gallery

To bring his "Indian Gallery" before the public, Catlin arranged for an exhibition in Pittsburgh as early as 1833. His collection was by no means complete; not until 1837 was a more comprehensive showing held in New York City at Clinton Hall. More exhibitions were held in various cities, including Boston, Philadelphia, and Washington.

Two years later, Catlin took his gallery, together with many items of Indian culture (altogether eight tons of it) to London. He took every conceivable article of Indian use —weapons, tools, costumes, and ceremonial items. In addition, there was a full-sized buffalo-hide tipi. At first, he dressed mannequins in the costumes. But Catlin was a showman. Next, he brought live Indians who sang and danced and did pantomimes of battle scenes and the hunt. His gallery and his show enthralled the people of England for nearly five years. His learned lectures earned him a high place in the social circles of London. Wined and dined, he was a popular luminary of the time.

In 1845, at the invitation of King Louis Philippe, Catlin moved his gallery to the Louvre in Paris. Here the French received him with the same acclaim as had the British. Catlin, was, in fact, an early and vastly colorful combination of Barnum and Buffalo Bill.

Catlin's Writings

In addition to his gallery and his early Wild West Show, Catlin devoted substantial energies to his writings. It was in 1841 that his *Letters and Notes on the Manners, Customs and Conditions of the North American Indians* was published. This two-volume work, reprinted several times, combined a travelog and anthropological observations. Illustrated with colored plates, most of these little line drawings were copies of the paintings in his gallery and are rendered with more clarity of detail and spontaneity of action than the original oils. This is particularly true of the scenes of village life, buffalo hunts, and landscapes. The year 1844 saw the publication of the *Indian Portfolio*, a collection of twenty-five hand-colored engravings.

Catlin's *Letters*, telling of his adventures and of Indian life, brought to the public one of the first detailed and illustrated descriptions of the Far West. While his travels were all for the purpose of achieving his main goal — painting Indians and preserving their history — his *Letters* are also filled with tales of narrow escapes, dangerous hunting escapades, arduous trips, and marvelous descriptions of the natural wonders and the wildlife he encountered.

His description of the prairie fire is a fair example of his observation. "The prairies burning form some of the most beautiful scenes that are to be witnessed in this country, and also some of the most sublime. Every acre of these vast prairies (being covered for hundreds and hundreds of miles, with a crop of grass, which dies and dries in the fall) burns over during the fall or early in the spring, leaving the ground of a black and doleful colour.

"There are many modes by which the fire is communicated to them, both by white men and by Indians —*par accident*; and yet many more where it is voluntarily done for the purpose of getting a fresh crop of grass, for the grazing of their horses, and also for easier travelling during the next summer, when there will be no old grass to lie upon the prairies, entangling the feet of man and horse, as they are passing over them.

"Over the elevated lands and prairie bluffs, where the grass is thin and short, the fire slowly creeps with a feeble flame, which one can easily step over; where the wild animals often rest in their lairs until the flames almost burn their noses, when they will reluctantly rise, and leap over it, and trot off amongst the cinders, where the fire has past and left the ground black as jet. These scenes at night become indescribably beautiful, when their flames are seen at many miles distance, creeping over the sides and tops of the bluffs, appearing to be sparkling and brilliant chains of liquid fire (the hills being lost to the view), hanging suspended in graceful festoons from the skies.

"But there is yet another character of burning prairies that requires another Letter, and a different pen to describe — the war, or hell of fires! where the grass is seven or eight feet high, as is often the case for many miles together, on the Missouri bottoms; and the flames are driven forward by the hurricanes, which often sweep over the vast prairies of this denuded country. There are many of the meadows on the Missouri, the Platte, and the Arkansas, of many miles in breadth, which are perfectly level, with a waving grass, so high, that we are obliged to stand erect in our stirrups, in order to look over its waving tops, as we are riding through it. The fire in these, before such a wind, travels at an immense and frightful rate, and often destroys, on their fleetest horses, parties of Indians, who are so unlucky as to be overtaken by it; not that it travels as fast as a horse at full speed, but that the high grass is filled with wild pea-vines and other impediments, which render it necessary for the rider to guide his horse in the zig-zag paths of the deers and buffaloes, retarding his progress, until he is overtaken by the dense column of smoke that is swept before the fire — alarming the horse, which stops and stands terrified and immutable, till the burning grass which is wafted in the wind, fall about him, kindling up in a moment a thousand new fires, which are instantly wrapped in the swelling flood of smoke that is moving on like a black thunder-cloud, rolling on the earth, with its lightning's glare, and its thunder rumbling as it goes."[12]

The Buffalo

Catlin wrote a considerable amount on the buffalo and their habits, and for such observations he is to be credited as one of the pioneer students of American wildlife. Typical of his writings is the account of the buffalo at bay.

"The white wolves, of which I have spoken in a former epistle, follow the herds of buffaloes as I have said, from one season to another, glutting themselves on the carcasses of those that fall by the deadly shafts of their enemies, or linger with disease or old age to be dispatched by these sneaking cormorants, who are ready at all time kindly to relieve them from the pangs of a lingering death.

"Whilst the herd is together, the wolves never attack them, as they instantly gather for combined resistance, which they effectually make. But when the herds are travelling, it often happens that an aged or wounded one, lingers at a distance behind, and when fairly out of sight of the herd, is set upon by these voracious hunters, which often gather to the number of fifty or more, and are sure at least to torture him to death, and use him up at a meal. The buffalo, however, is a huge and furious animal, and when his retreat is cut off, makes desperate and deadly resistance, contending to the last moment for the right of life — and oftentimes deals death by wholesale, to his canine assailants, which he is tossing into the air or stamping to death under his feet."[13]

Indian Life

Most significant, however, are the author's observations of Indian life. Many of his ethnographical descriptions are classic firsts in our knowledge of

Indian culture. Catlin's portrayal of the Mandans' O-Kee-Pa ceremony is noteworthy reporting. His introductory remarks explain its purpose quite well.

"The Mandans believe in the existence of a Great (or Good) Spirit, and also of an Evil Spirit, who they say existed long before the Good Spirit, and is far superior in power. They all believe also in a future state of existence, and a future administration of rewards and punishments, and (as do all other tribes that I have yet visited) they believe those punishments are not eternal, but commensurate with their sins.

"These people, living in a climate where they suffer from cold in the severity of their winter, have very naturally reversed our ideas of Heaven and Hell. The latter they describe to be a country very far to the north, of barren and hideous aspect, and covered with eternal snows and ice. The torments of this freezing place they describe· as most excruciating; whilst Heaven they suppose to be in a warmer and delightful latitude, where nothing is felt but the keenest enjoyment and where the country abounds in buffaloes and other luxuries of life. The Great or Good Spirit they believe dwells in the former place, [Catlin means hell], for the purpose of there meeting those who have offended him; increasing the agony of the sufferings, by being himself present, administering the penalties. The Bad or Evil Spirit they at the same time suppose to reside in Paradise, still tempting the happy; and those who have gone to the regions of punishment they believe to be tortured for a time proportioned to the amount of their transgressions, and that they are again liable to the temptations of the Evil Spirit, and answerable again at a future period for their new offences.

"Such is the religious creed of the Mandans, and for the purpose of appeasing the Good and Evil Spirits, and to secure their entrance into those 'fields Elysian', or beautiful hunting grounds, do the young men subject themselves to the horrid and sickening cruelties to be described in the following pages.

[Catlin is referring to the torture features of the ceremony.]

"There are other three distinct objects (yet to be named) for which these religious ceremonies are held, which are as follows:

"*First*, they are held annually as a celebration of the event of the subsiding of the Flood, which they call *Mee-nee-ro-ka-ha-sha* (sinking down or settling of the waters).

"*Secondly,* for the purpose of dancing what they call, *Bel-lohck-na-pic* (the bull-dance); to the strict observance of which they attribute the coming of buffaloes to supply them with food during the season; and

"*Thirdly* and lastly, for the purpose of conducting all the young men of the tribe, as they annually arrive to the age of manhood, through an ordeal of privation and torture, which, while it is supposed to harden their muscles and prepare them for extreme endurance, enables the chiefs who are spectators to the scene, to decide upon their comparative bodily strength and ability to endure the extreme privations and sufferings that often fall to the lots of Indian warriors; and that they may decide who is the most hardy and best able to lead a war-party in case of extreme exigency."[14]

In telling of the Indians' belief in and dependence upon supernatural power, Catlin explained it quite adequately:

"The 'medicine-bag' then, is a mystery-bag; and its meaning and importance necessary to be understood, as it may be said to be the key of Indian life and Indian character. These bags are constructed of the skins of animals, birds, or of reptiles, and ornamented and preserved in a thousand different ways, as suits the taste or freak of the person who constructs them. These skins are generally attached to some part of the clothing of the Indian, or carried in his hand — they are oftentimes decorated in such a manner as to be exceedingly ornamental to his person, and always are stuffed with grass, or moss, or something of the kind; and generally without drugs or medicines within them, as they are religiously closed and sealed and seldom, if ever, to be opened. I find that every

Indian in his primitive state, carries his medicine-bag in some form or other, to which he pays the greatest homage, and to which he looks for safety and protection through life — and in fact, it might almost be called a species of idolatry; for it would seem in some instances, as if he actually worshipped it. Feasts are often made, and dogs and horses sacrificed, to a man's medicine; and days, and even weeks, of fasting and penance of various kinds are often suffered, to appease his medicine, which he imagines he has in some way offended.

"The manner in which this curious and important article is instituted is this: a boy, at the age of fourteen or fifteen years, is said to be making or 'forming his medicine,' when he wanders away from his father's lodge, and absents himself for the space of two or three, sometimes even four or five days; lying on the ground in some remote or secluded spot, crying to the Great Spirit, and fasting the whole time. During this period of peril and abstinence, when he falls asleep, the first animal, bird, or reptile, of which he dreams (or pretends to have dreamed, perhaps), he considers the Great Spirit has designated for his mysterious protector through life. He then returns home to his father's lodge, and relates his success; and after allaying his thirst, and satiating his appetite, he sallies forth with weapons or traps, until he can procure the animal or bird, the skin of which he preserves entire, and ornaments it according to his own fancy, and carries it with him through life, for 'good luck' (as he calls it); as his strength in battle — and in death his guardian *Spirit* that is buried with him; and which is to conduct him safe to the beautiful hunting grounds, which he contemplates in the world to come."[15]

Catlin wrote about the Indians with a heartfelt respect and compassion rare for his time. About the only feature he found disgusting was the torture in the Mandan O-Kee-Pa ceremony and he wrote objectively even of this. Of Indians in general, he had this comment:

"From what I have seen of these people I feel authorized to say, that there is nothing very strange or unaccountable in their character; but that it is a simple one, and easy to be learned and understood, if the right means be taken to familiarise ourselves with it. Although it has its dark spots; yet there is much in it to be applauded, and much to recommend it to the admiration of the enlightened world. And I trust that the reader, who looks through these volumes with care, will be disposed to join me in the conclusion: that the North American Indian in his native state is an honest, hospitable, faithful, brave, warlike, cruel, revengeful, relentless — yet honourable, contemplative and religious being."[16]

Catlin's Theories

While Catlin's reporting was accurate in most cases, some of his theorizing was fanciful. He was struck by certain beliefs and ceremonial symbols held in common by Indians and Jews. Among the supposed similarities was the wearing of horned headdresses by the bravest of warriors, a custom Catlin believed to have been "handed down and preserved with very little innovation or change from that ancient time."

Catlin was especially impressed by the Mandans, believing them to be a superior tribe among the many he had visited. He singled out their Second Chief, Mah-to-toh-pa, as the outstanding Indian on the continent. Partly because of the complexity of their culture and partly because of the genetic albinism found among many of the women, which produced a silvery blond quality in the hair and, in some instances, blue eyes, Catlin had a theory that these people were intermixed with the descendants of Prince Madoc's lost Welsh colony. He took some pains to explore this premise, even to the extent of mapping what he presumed to be earlier earth lodge village sites as far east as the Ohio River. In addition, he used certain cultural traits, such as the making of pottery and glass beads, as well as the similarity of certain Mandan and Welsh words, as indicators of the relationship.

The facts, however, do not yet bear him out. Achromatrichia, or the absence of pigmentation, causing prematurely gray hair, was not confined to the Mandans; both sexes were subject to it, but the men dyed their hair.

Historical and archaeological evidence indicates that many tribes built earth lodges, and while the Mandans had moved their villages in earlier times, the Ohio River settlements belong to another people. The making of pottery was universal among the sedentary eastern, Mississippi, and Missouri River tribes, though the making of glazed beads among the Mandans may have been unique. Similarities in vocabulary would appear to be coincidental and Catlin's examples often appear to stretch the point. The high cultural plane which Catlin accords the Mandans, as opposed to a lower state for the other tribes he visited, is not justified. Many groups had an equally complex culture. Catlin spent many days at the Mandan villages — more time than with any other groups of Indians — and understandably, he was overly impressed.

Authenticity

Catlin was concerned that the public might not accept his paintings as accurate portrayals of Indian life. Some of the things that Catlin saw and depicted were startling and unbelievable. To authenticate his paintings, he took the trouble to obtain signed certifications from respected Indian agents and fur company representatives, including William Clark. A typical example of such a document said: "I have seen Mr. Catlin's Collection of Indian Portraits, many of which were familiar to me, and painted in my presence at their own villages. I have spent the greater part of my life amongst the tribes and individuals he has represented, and I do not hesitate or pronounce them correct likenesses and easily recognized; also his sketches of the *manners* and *customs*, I think, are excellent; and

the *landscape views* on the Missouri and Mississippi, are correct representations. K. McKenzie, *of the Am. Fur Co. Mouth of the Yellowstone.*"

Despite these precautions, Catlin did not escape being called a fraud by some. Henry Schoolcraft, the American ethnologist, denounced Catlin's paintings and text of the Mandan O-Kee-Pa ceremony as fakes, although Catlin has long been vindicated.

While Catlin's writings constitute an invaluable ethnographic contribution, his *Letters* are confused and disorganized. Although they are numbered from 1 to 58, in all too many instances the numbers bear no relation to actual sequence. Dates are so sparingly used that it is impossible to tell where Catlin was at any given time. He constantly refers his readers to past occurrences or to observations in former *Letters*, or promises the reader to explore a topic in a future "epistle," but sometimes fails to do it. His total disregard for systematic writing makes for frustrating reading indeed.

Final Years

Artist, author, and showman that he was, Catlin was not fortunate with his money. His last year in London, 1848, found him in financial difficulties. Attendance at his exhibition was falling off, and he was in debt. It was after several of his belongings were put on the auction block to satisfy his creditors that a wealthy Philadelphian, Joseph Harrison, saved Catlin from ruin by paying off his obligations and taking over the Indian Gallery.

This fiasco, however, did not deter Catlin. Now he began writing books. In 1851 he was commissioned to paint 56 copies of his original at $2.00 each for Sir Thomas Phillips and was later commissioned to do 107 pencil drawings. From 1853 to 1858 he engaged in various extensive tours of South America, the Pacific Northwest, the Rocky Mountains, California, and the desert Southwest. In 1860 he began feverishly copying his works on cardboard and adding paintings of his trips to South America and the Pacific Northwest. His hope was to sell his collection to the Government, but this hope was unfulfilled. Impoverished, he died on December 28, 1872, in Jersey City, New Jersey at the age of seventy-five.

The owner of Catlin's Gallery, Mr. Harrison, had also died, but his widow retained the collection. In 1879 Thomas Donaldson heard of its whereabouts and, together with the Secretary of the Smithsonian Institution, inspected it. It was Donaldson who persuaded Mrs. Harrison to donate the collection, and she graciously agreed. Thanks to her generosity, Catlin's Indian Gallery now hangs in the National Collection of Fine Arts in Washington, D.C.

The Indians

Since Catlin's time, historians and anthropologists have gathered voluminous material about the American Indians, so that today we know a great deal more concerning the Native Americans' life styles than Catlin could possibly have obtained. To put his paintings and observations in perspective, a section dealing exclusively with the Indian way of life is included here. Rather than looking at Catlin's subjects in a vacuum, they now may be better viewed in the context of their cultural setting.

The North American Indians whom Catlin painted came from a variety of cultures and life styles. Catlin reported these differences to a degree, but his main purpose was to paint a dramatic panorama of the Native American, accentuating the striking differences between Indian customs and those of "civilized society." In this he did a most sympathetic job. But the study of the cultural traits and culture areas was not developed until the twentieth century. The result is that Catlin did not differentiate, for example, between Woodland and Plains peoples and their ways of life.

The Eastern Woodlands actually comprised a vast area stretching from Florida to southern Canada, and west beyond the Great Lakes and the Mississippi River. Here lived agricultural people whose women farmed the fields of corn, beans, and squash. For the most part, theirs was a sedentary life, punctuated by ceremonies, war, and the hunt. Villages consisted of wattle and daub houses in the south and bark-covered wigwams in the north. Nearly all were stockaded. Among such southern Indians as the Choctaws, Creeks, Seminoles, and Cherokees, there had developed highly ritualized societies. Theocratic in character, they were led by princely priests. Temple mounds dominated the central plazas of the towns. Wars of retaliation were incessant; booty and tribute were the victors' rewards.

To the north were the Iroquois, the Delawares and Shawnees, the Ottowas, the Mohegans, and the Illinois. As an example of Northeastern woodland life, the Iroquois are worthy of note. Arriving from the south, they drove a wedge between the Algonquian-speaking Shawnees, Susquehannas, Delawares, and Mohegans to the east and the Miamis, Illinois, and Eries to the west. In what is now New York State, they established a league composed of the Senecas, Cayugas, and Onondagas to the west and the Oneidas and Mohawks to the east. With the arrival of the Tuscaroras in the eighteenth century, they were known as the Six Nations and became the most powerful political Indian force in Colonial America.

Theirs was a sophisticated government, wherein clan mothers nominated *sachems* who met in council. The people were divided into clans: the Bear, the Deer, the Wolf, and so on. Descent was reckoned from the mother, yet in marriage, one had to choose a spouse from outside one's clan. In this matriarchy, the husband moved to his wife's family lodge. The women arranged the marriages, often choosing an older man for a younger woman, an older woman for a younger man. In this way, young spouses were always assured of an experienced partner.

The women's role in Iroquois society was a powerful one. Not only did they arrange marriages, they owned the bark-covered houses, all the utensils, the fields, and the harvests, determined who would be *sachems*, and held the power to depose them.

Stockaded villages were surrounded by fields where the women farmed. The men were the hunters and warriors, the shamans, priests, and councilmen. Wars of conquest were commonplace to the extent that the Iroquois completely dominated the entire region. During the American Revolution, the Senecas, Onondagas, Cayugas, and Tuscaroras sided with the British to pillage and burn the American settlements and take the inhabitants captive. Not until John Sullivan's troops successfully burned all the Iroquois towns and crops in 1779 did the ravages cease. No longer were the Iroquois a power to be feared; their influence had been crushed.

The woodland culture spread throughout the Great Lakes area and through all the Midwest to the Missouri River. Peoples like the Menominee and Sac and Fox to the north and the Oto and Osage to the south practiced an agricultural and hunting economy similar to their eastern neighbors. The women were the farmers, while the men hunted, dominated the ceremonial life, and made war.

The allied tribes of the Sac and Fox offer a typical example of this way of life. Like all woodland people, they placed their villages near the rivers, for the waterways were the Indians' highways. Women tilled the fields, which were sometimes as large as 100 acres. The land was rich in wild fruits and berries, which the women gathered. In the spring, maple trees were tapped for their syrup. When fall arrived, the Sac and Fox left their towns, going west to the prairielands in search of buffalo and elk. Returning to their villages when winter approached, they sat snug around the fire, relating tales and myths.

Each tribe was split into two divisions and, in turn, each division was composed of several clans such as the Sturgeon, the Bear, or the Thunder. Descent was from the father's line and with it came valuable properties and important religious rights. Among these were sacred bundles or medicine bags containing objects received as a kind of totem in a vision. On auspicious occasions, such as spring planting or fall harvest, the bundles were ceremonially opened by the clan keepers amidst song and dance and prayer.

At birth, the parents designated boy babies a color, perhaps black for the firstborn, white for the second. This designation was retained through life and determined which team one played on in the ball game, which is now called lacrosse. Young men were expected to seek visions in order to gain power. Some gained exceptional supernatural force and became shamans. Such men could cure sickness, foretell future events, and find lost articles.

As early as 1804, whites were pressuring the Sac and Fox for their lands. The Indians signed away their holdings under threat of military destruction and moved west of the Mississippi. Under the leadership of Black Hawk, a group of Sacs refused to accept the terms. Enlisting the aid of Creeks, Cherokees, Winnebagos, and Osages, Black Hawk led 500 warriors back to his homeland. Skirmishes ensued and his allies fell away. In an attempt to surrender, Black Hawk's peace emissaries were shot down. Outraged, he attacked the white forces with some success. Retreating north, pursued by the militia and a party of Sioux, he surrendered under a white flag. But his gesture was ignored, and his band was mercilessly slaughtered — men, women, and children. Black Hawk escaped, but was shortly captured and imprisoned. However, the next year, 1833, he was released to return to Iowa among his saddened people.

The Great Plains was an unending sea of grass, stretching westward from the Missouri River to the Rocky Mountains. Once huge herds of buffalo roamed these barren, windswept lands, and many Indians depended upon these animals for their livelihood. Some, like the Pawnees, Wichitas, Arikaras, and Mandans were also farmers, living in great stockaded earth-lodge villages along the riverbanks. Others, including the Comanches, Kiowas, Cheyennes, Crows, Blackfeet, and Sioux were entirely nomadic, depending upon the buffalo for their support.

Far up the Missouri River, near what is now Bismarck, North Dakota, lived the Mandans. High above the river, they were secure against their enemies. The Mandans believed that "Wakonda," the all-powerful Sun, imbued men with this power through animal emissaries. The surest way to achieve this source of strength and to accomplish life's goals — success in war, in the hunt, in curing the sick, and in achieving high status among one's fellowmen — was to undergo self-torture in the annual O-Kee-Pa ceremony. Under the supervision of mentor-priests, young men endured the piercing of skewers through their chest and back muscles. Thongs were attached to the skewers and then drawn over the beams in the ceremonial earth-lodge. Next, the participants were pulled up so they hung suspended by the ropes several feet from the ground. During the torture, songs were sung by the spectators. The ordeal might last several hours until the supplicants tore themselves loose. Though painful, this was the surest way to communicate directly with Wakonda.

The head men of the Mandans chose from among themselves a War Chief, a Peace Chief, and a Village Chief. Men achieved these positions because of their ability in war, in the hunt, and in the exhibition of their wisdom and power. It was during council meetings that the pipe was smoked. Smoking was considered proper supplication to the gods and it was the tobacco smoke that would convey the Indians' appeals.

The Mandans were once a prosperous people, living in as many as thirteen villages with an estimated population of 3,600. They divided themselves into two moieties — the Lefts and the Rights. Within each division were several clans, and representatives of every clan could be found in each village. Inheritance was reckoned from the mother, and in marriage one had to choose a spouse from outside his or her clan, as well as from the other moiety.

Smallpox struck the Mandans in the eighteenth century so that they were reduced to two villages by the time of Catlin's visit in the early nineteenth century. Racked by cholera, syphilis, the measles, and always smallpox, by the middle of the nineteenth century they numbered no more than thirty-nine ragged, impoverished remnants of a once proud nation.

Among the most dramatic of all American Indians were the nomadic buffalo hunters, and none captured the imagination more than the Sioux. These warlike horsemen destroyed General Custer's ambitions for the Presidency and alerted the nation to the Indians' determination to preserve their way of life.

Living in portable buffalo-hide tipis, they did no farming, but lived solely on the buffalo and on the wild fruits, vegetables, and berries gathered by the women. Wealth, for the Sioux, consisted of horses, and raiding parties constantly left the camps with the idea of capturing these animals from the enemies' villages. The man with the most horses lived in the largest tipis and had the most wives. But the mere accumulation of horses did not assure status. Only by distributing them as gifts did one achieve high position.

For the Sioux, war was a kind of game in which men gained "coups" or points for striking the enemy. War records were kept, and the man with the greatest number was accorded high status. Scalps were trophies of victory, but they were even more than that. The Sioux believed that human hair was equated with the soul, indicated by the fact of its continuing growth after death. When a relative was killed and scalped in battle, it was believed that his spirit could not enter the "Land Beyond" until another scalp was taken in order to bring together the slain relative and his hair. Warriors would thereby go to battle to acquire a scalp and bring it home to the mother or sister of the one killed, saying: "Here is your son. Rejoice, his spirit and body are now one. He may now go to the 'Land of Many Lodges.' Sing and dance and be happy."

Like the Mandans, the Sioux believed that power was acquired from the supernatural through visions. The most effective way to gain power was to endure the tortures of the Sun Dance. Here young men were suspended from a pole by thongs and skewers thrust through their chests. Those who underwent this ordeal became shamans and priests, pledged to do good for others and to care for their spiritual needs.

While Catlin's goal was to portray all the Indians, in gathering his gallery he had no opportunity at this time to reach the Southwest and paint the Pueblos in their adobe villages.

Nor was he able to paint the Navahos or Apaches; under Mexican control, the Southwest was a region closed to him. Nor did he obtain portraits of the California Indians. This, however, in no way invalidates his monumental achievement or the value of his contributions. He recorded what was available to him, and in doing so he accomplished a masterpiece.

Altogether Catlin painted representatives of fifty-five tribes comprising about two-thirds the number residing in what was then the United States and its territories. And to accomplish this he traveled widely throughout Indian country, particularly west of the Mississippi River, where the Indians were still living in their native state. As a result Catlin produced the largest and most comprehensive record of the American West the nation had ever seen. This prodigious accomplishment is not only a tribute to his dedication but an inestimable contribution to the nation's understanding of the Native American's heritage.

NOTES

All quotations from Catlin's writings are from George Catlin, *Letters and Notes on the Manners, Customs and Conditions of the North American Indians.* 2 Volumes (London, 1841).

1. Volume One, page 2
2. Volume One, page 4
3. Volume Two, page 246
4. Volume Two, page 111
5. Volume Two, page 26
6. Volume Two, page 28
7. Volume One, page 26
8. Volume One, page 91
9. Volume Two, page 46
10. Volume Two, page 51
11. Volume One, page 254
12. Volume Two, page 19
13. Volume One, page 289
14. Volume One, page 177
15. Volume One, page 41
16. Volume One, page 9

THE AMERICAN INDIANS

ARIKARA	MISSOURI
ASSINIBOINE	MOHEGAN
BLACKFEET	OMAHA
CHEROKEE	OSAGE
CHEYENNE	OTTAWA
CHIPPEWA	OTO
CHOCKTAW	PAWNEE
COMMANCHE	PEORIA
CREEK	PIANKASHAW
CROW	PLAINS CREE
DELAWARE	PLAINS OJIBWA
HIDATSA	PONCA
IOWA	SAC AND FOX
IROQUOIS	SANTEE SIOUX
KANSAS	SEMINOLE
KASKASKIA	SHAWNEE
KICKAPOO	TETON SIOUX
KIOWA	YANKTON SIOUX
MANDAN	WEA
MENOMINEE	WICHITA
MINNESOTA	WINNEBAGO

THE LICKER
Seminole, 1838, oil on canvas, 29″ x 24″ (74 x 61 cm).
Commonly called "Creek Billy," he was considered an outstanding warrior and "a very handsome fellow." The Seminoles whom Catlin painted were captives, of which there were about 200.

OSCEOLA, NICK-A-NO-CHEE
Seminole, 1840?, oil on canvas, 52″ x 40″ (132 x 102 cm).
This Seminole boy was about ten years old. Suspended from his neck are three silver gorgets,
18th century military vestiges of medieval armor.

A SEMINOLE WOMAN
1838, oil on canvas, 29″ x 24″ (74 x 61 cm).

The girl here is shown wearing silver brooches on her blouse. The Seminoles, an offshoot of the Southern Creeks, inhabited the Everglades of Florida.

TEL-MAZ-HA-ZA
Creek, 1834, oil on canvas, 29″ x 24″ (74 x 61 cm).
Since the Creeks had formerly kept slaves and welcomed escaped blacks to their fold, there was considerable racial intermixture. This may account for this warrior's mustache and beard.

DRINKS THE JUICE OF THE STONE
Choctaw, 1834, oil on canvas, 29" x 24" (74 x 61 cm).
Here the most outstanding ball player of the tribe wears the official costume of the game: a huge tail of white horsehair and a dyed cape of the same.

BALL PLAY OF THE CHOCTAW — BALL UP
1834-35, oil on canvas, 19½″ x 27⅜″ (48 x 70 cm).

Each player carried two sticks in this original version of lacrosse. There were literally no boundaries, so players might run for several miles before returning to attempt to score a goal.

COL-LE
Cherokee, 1834, oil on canvas, 29″ x 24″ (74 x 61 cm).

Catlin noted the intermixture of white and Indian blood among the Cherokee. His portrait of their head chief clearly indicates this fact.

THE OPEN DOOR
Shawnee, 1830, oil on canvas, 29″ x 24″ (74 x 61 cm).

Twin brother of Tecumseh, he was known as "The Prophet." With his sacred string of beads and "fire stick," acquired through a vision, he and his brother tried to ally all the Indian nations, from Florida to the headwaters of the Missouri River, in order to drive the white settlers east of the Ohio River. Blind in the left eye, he was in his early sixties at the time of this portrait.

STRAIGHT MAN
Shawnee, 1830, oil on canvas, 29″ x 24″ (74 x 61 cm).
This noted Shawnee warrior had distinguished himself by his exploits. Catlin remarks about his unusual red and black face paint.

GOES UP THE RIVER
Shawnee, 1830, oil on canvas, 29″ x 24″ (74 x 61 cm).
This chief of the Shawnees has slit the rims of his ears, on which rings are hung, a fashion popular among this tribe.

BOD-A-SIN
Delaware, 1830, oil on canvas, 29″ x 24″ (74 x 61 cm).
This chief is not mentioned in Catlin's Letters. *By now, the Delawares had adopted much of the white man's dress.*

NON-ON-DA-GON
Delaware, 1830, oil on canvas, 29″ x 24″ (74 x 61 cm).
*Catlin became very fond of the gentlemanly chief with the silver nose ring. From his portrait,
he was apparently a huge man, if not obese.*

STANDS BY HIMSELF
Wea, 1830, oil on canvas, 29″ x 24″ (74 x 61 cm).

Once a powerful Indian tribe, the Weas were reduced to a mere 200 people. This man was described by Catlin as having an "intelligent European head."

CUSICK
Iroquois, 1837-39, oil on canvas, 29″ x 24″ (74 x 61 cm).
Son of the chief of the Tuscaroras, this well-educated man was an eloquent Baptist preacher.

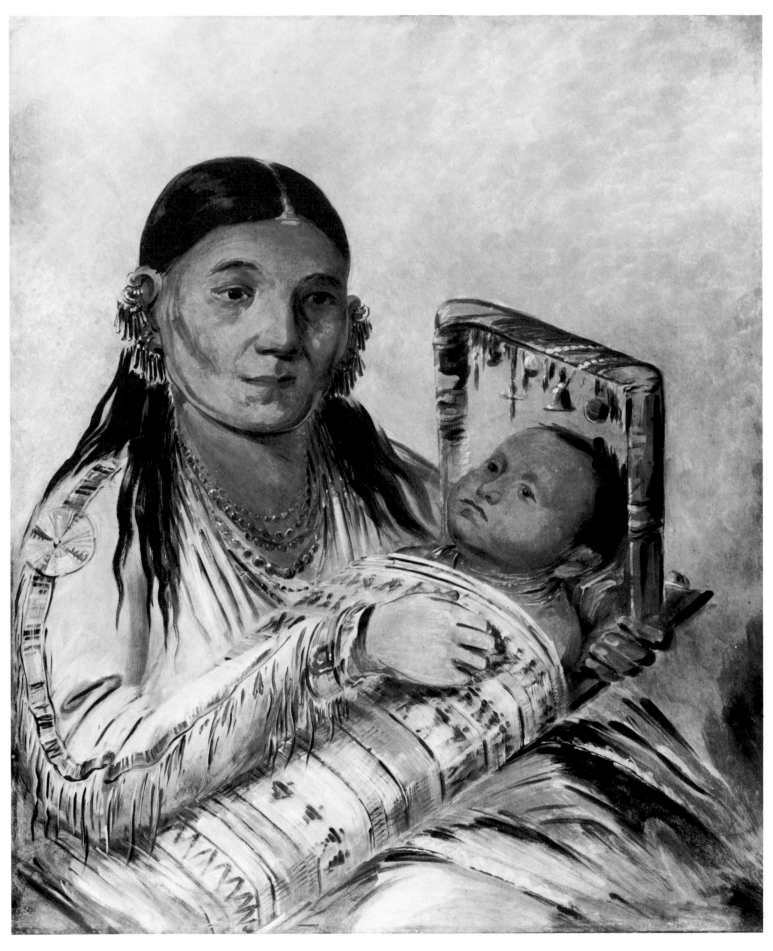

CHE-AH-KA-TCHEE
Iroquois, 1835-36, oil on canvas, 29″ x 24″ (74 x 61 cm).
Wife of Not-To-Way, she holds her child in a cradle board.

NOT-TO-WAY
Iroquois, 1835-36, oil on canvas, 29" x 24" (74 x 61 cm).
This chief, named "The Thinker," though "an excellent man," according to Catlin, was
"quite ignorant of the history of his people."

DEEP LAKE
Iroquois, 1831, oil on canvas, 21⅛" x 16½" (54 x 42 cm).
This old Seneca sachem was leader of the "Great Hill People." The Senecas were the "Keepers of the Western Door" of the Five Nations of the Iroquois League.

BREAD
Iroquois, 1830, oil on canvas, 21½″ x 16½″ (54 x 42 cm).
*This chief of the Oneida impressed Catlin: a "shrewd and talented man, well educated —
speaking good English — is handsome, and a polite and gentlemanly man in his deportment."*

BIG SAIL
Ottawa, 1836, oil on canvas, 29″ x 24″ (74 x 61 cm).
This Canadian Chief wears a peace medal, probably British. The Ottawa, known as the "Traders," lived north of Lake Huron and did their trading at Fort Michilimackinac.

LITTLE CHIEF
Kaskaskia, 1830, oil on canvas, 29″ x 24″ (74 x 61 cm).

The Kaskaskias, members of the once great Illinois Confederacy, were so reduced in numbers that the traders told Catlin that Little Chief was the leader of only two people: his mother and his son.

MAN WHO TRACKS
Peoria, 1830, oil on canvas, 29" x 24" (74 x 61 cm).

The Peoria were one of the principal tribes of the Illinois Confederacy. By Catlin's time, this chief had no more than 200 tribesmen remaining.

NO ENGLISH

Peoria, 1830, oil on canvas, 29″ x 24″ (74 x 61 cm).

Said to be one of the most influential men of his tribe, he was considered a dandy. No English is shown here holding a prayer stick.

THE FOREMOST MAN
Kickapoo, 1831, oil on canvas, 29″ x 24″ (74 x 61 cm).
This chief, a shrewd and talented man, was referred to as the "Prophet." He embraced Christianity and held services regularly on Sundays.

FIX WITH THE FOOT
Piankashaw, 1830, oil on canvas, 29″ x 24″ (74 x 61 cm).

*By the time Catlin painted this brave of distinction, the tribe was reduced to a mere 170
persons. The Piankashaws were a division of the Miamis, living south of Lake Michigan.*

THE SPANIARD
Winnebago, 1828, oil on canvas, 18½" x 14⅛" (47 x 36 cm).

As opposed to Catlin's rendering of the "Boxer," which follows, this man appears to be too much head and too little body.

HE WHO MOISTENS THE WOOD
Winnebago, 1836?, oil on canvas, 18½″ x 14⅛″ (47 x 36 cm).
This sketch captures Catlin's description of the Winnebago physique. Apparently, the Winnebagos liked to pose in warlike postures.

MAN WHO PUTS ALL OUT OF DOORS
Winnebago, 1835, oil on canvas, 29″ x 24″ (74 x 61 cm).

Known as the "Boxer," he was the largest man in the tribe. Catlin's portrait conveys his size, but surely he was not the pinhead that the artist's out-of-drawing picture implies. Suspended from the subject's arms are rattlesnake skins.

BOTH SIDES OF THE RIVER
Mohegan, 1831, oil on canvas, 29" x 24" (74 x 61 cm).
Originally from Connecticut, this chief was painted at Green Bay, where 400 remnants of the Mohegans had been moved. The subject is shown here holding a prayer book.

WIFE OF KEOKUK
Sac and Fox, 1835; oil on canvas, 29" x 24" (74 x 61 cm).
One of seven wives, she was Keokuk's favorite. Her elegant costume consists of a wraparound skirt, decorated with appliqued ribbon work, and a blouse richly covered with silver brooches.

THE WHALE
Sac and Fox, 1834, oil on canvas, 29″ x 24″ (74 x 61 cm).
One of Keokuk's principal braves, he is shown wearing a crow bustle at his waist.

DEER'S HAIR
Sac and Fox, 1834, oil on canvas, 29" x 24" (74 x 61 cm).

Keokuk's favorite son, whom he expected to succeed him, is shown here wearing a small bear-claw necklace, which he scarcely could have earned.

KEOKUK
Sac and Fox, 1835, oil on canvas, 29″ x 24″ (74 x 61 cm).
"The Watchful Fox," chief of the Sac and Fox, held two-thirds of his warriors neutral in the "Black Hawk War." His eloquence as a public speaker was renowned.

WHITE CLOUD
Sac and Fox, 1832, oil on canvas, 29″ x 24″ (74 x 61 cm).
Confidant of Black Hawk, he was known as the "Prophet." At the time of his portrait, he was allowing his hair to grow in order to curry favor with the whites.

BLACK HAWK
Sac and Fox, 1832, oil on canvas, 29″ x 24″ (74 x 61 cm).
Leader of a fateful, last-ditch attempt to unite the Indian tribes in driving away the whites,
he was defeated by General Atkinson and held prisoner of war.

KEOKUK ON HORSEBACK
Sac and Fox, 1834, 24″ x 29″ (61 x 74 cm).

Keokuk insisted that Catlin paint him on horseback to please his vanity. His horse was considered the best animal on the frontier, a blooded steed which had cost $300.

GRIZZLY BEAR
Menominee, 1831, oil on canvas, 21⅛" x 16 7/16" (54 x 43 cm).
This man once led fifteen of his tribesmen to Washington and "there commanded great respect for his eloquence, and dignity of deportment."

SAM PERRYMAN

Creek, 1834, oil on canvas, 29″ x 24″ (74 x 61 cm).

Brother of the "Great King" of the Creeks, he too was a high-ranking member of this nation. Catlin was impressed by the "picturesque taste" of Creek costumes.

TCHOW-EE-PUT-O-KAW
Creek, 1836, oil on canvas, 29″ x 24″ (74 x 61 cm).
While most of the Creeks had adopted European dress, this woman's costume appears to be of native make. Her necklace of silver discs may have been a trade item.

BALL PLAY OF THE CHOCTAW — BALL UP
1834-35, oil on canvas, 19½″ x 27⅝″ (50 x 70 cm).

*Compared with the earlier illustration of the lacrosse game, this is an example of Catlin's
tendency to make copies of his works. This appears to be a more finished version.*

SNAPPING TURTLE
Choctaw, 1834, oil on canvas, 29″ x 24″ (74 x 61 cm).
Distinguished, gentlemanly, and well-educated, he was known to the whites as Peter Pinchlin. He gave Catlin much information about the history and traditions of his tribe.

LITTLE WOLF
Iowa, 1844, oil on canvas, 29″ x 24″ (74 x 61 cm).
This warrior is probably displaying his war paint. Such painting was usually prescribed by a shaman as a protective device against harm in battle.

HE WHO KILLS THE OSAGES
Missouri, 1832, oil on canvas, 29″ x 24″ (74 x 61 cm).
This aged chief holds an effigy pipe, carved from red pipestone or catlinite.

BIG ELK
Omaha, 1832, oil on canvas, 24″ x 24″ (61 x 61 cm).
This famous warrior is shown with his pipe-tomahawk, a popular trade item. His black face paint symbolizes his having just successfully killed an enemy in battle.

DOUBLE WALKER
Omaha, 1832, oil on canvas, 29″ x 24″ (74 x 61 cm).

This man's smoking mixture was probably an aromatic combination of dried willow bark, kinnikinnick, and tobacco.

THE BLACK COAT
Cherokee, 1836, oil on canvas, 29″ x 24″ (74 x 61 cm).
The Cherokee had adopted many white customs, as this chief's calico shirt indicates.

WAH-CHEE-TE AND CHILD
Osage, 1834, oil on canvas, 29″ x 24″ (74 x 61 cm).
The wife of Cleremont holds her child. Indian children seldom wore clothes until they were three or four years old. Catlin, however, describes the mother as dressed most lavishly in European attire, unusual since the Osages had strongly rejected "every luxury and every custom of civilized people."

OSCEOLA
Seminole, 1838, oil on canvas, 30⅞″ x 25⅞″ (78 x 66 cm).

Though not a chief, this Seminole leader was the most respected man in his tribe. His bravery, fortitude, and endurance were unsurpassed. This formal portrait is one of Catlin's finest.

COCK TURKEY
Kickapoo, 1831, oil on canvas, 29″ x 24″ (74 x 61 cm).
A disciple of the "Prophet," he is shown reciting his prayers with the aid of a prayer stick, upon which characters were engraved as memory aids.

DANCE TO THE BERDASHE
Sac and Fox, 1835-37, oil on canvas, 19⅝" x 27⅝" (50 x 70 cm).

The transvestite is honored annually by this dance, but the only dancers are men who have had relations with him. Living the life of women, transvestites were possessed of supernatural power or "strong medicine," but were ordinarily shunned.

DISCOVERY DANCE
Sac and Fox, 1835-37, 19½″ x 27½″ (50 x 70 cm).

With only the simultaneous patting of their feet on the ground, and in perfect time, the dancers mimicked the discovery of approaching game or enemies, reporting back to the leader of the dance.

THE IOWAY
Sac and Fox, 1832, oil on canvas, 29″ x 24″ (74 x 61 cm).

One of Black Hawk's principal warriors, he is described by Catlin as wearing his war paint, the hands probably indicating that he had conquered his enemy in hand-to-hand combat.

ROARING THUNDER
Sac and Fox, 1832, oil on canvas, 29″ x 24″ (74 x 61 cm).
This youngest son of Black Hawk was painted while a prisoner of war.

BEAR'S TRACK
Sac and Fox, 1835, oil on canvas, 29″ x 24″ (74 x 61 cm).
This man is wearing a "crow bustle," a fashionable item of ceremonial attire.

PORTRAIT OF TWO UNNAMED MEN
Menominee, 1835-36, oil on canvas, 29″ x 24″ (74 x 61 cm).
Catlin did not get the names of these young men. One holds a war club; the other is playing his "love flute," the magic notes of which attracted young women.

PASH-SHEE-NAU-SHAW
Menominee, 1831, oil on canvas, 21⅛″ x 16⅝″ (54 x 42 cm).
This young warrior is wearing a trade blanket. Catlin noted that the Menominee were out of the range of the buffalo, but formerly, they would have worn robes of deer skins.

MASH-KEE-WET
Menominee, 1831, oil on canvas, 21⅛″ x 16⅝″ (54 x 42 cm).
His name is translated "The Thought." He was considered to be a great dandy.

SMALL WHOOP
Menominee, 1831, oil on canvas, 21⅛″ x 16⅝″ (54 x 42 cm).
He is shown here wearing a peace medal and a metal star. The star seems to have been a very popular decoration among this tribe.

THE HAIL STORM
Chippewa, 1843, oil on canvas, 29″ x 24″ (74 x 61 cm).
This man sat for his portrait while on a tour in Europe.

SITS EVERYWHERE
Chippewa, 1835, oil on canvas, 29″ x 24″ (74 x 61 cm).
The metal armlets and bracelets were highly prized items of the trade.

JU-AH-KIS-GAW
Chippewa, 1835, oil on canvas, 29″ x 24″ (74 x 61 cm).
*Above the child's face dangle small bundles, one containing the infant's dried umbilicus as a
protective device.*

STRONG WIND
Chippewa, 1843, oil on canvas, 29" x 24" (74 x 61 cm).
This dignitary, wearing two peace medals, has painted a hand across his mouth, possibly indicating some warlike accomplishment.

THE OTTOWAY
Chippewa, 1835, oil on canvas, 29″ x 24″ (74 x 61 cm).
This distinguished warrior wears a huge necklace of brass and a bandolier, a very popular article among the eastern tribes.

NO HEART
Iowa, 1832, oil on canvas, 29" x 24" (74 x 61 cm).

Chief of the tribe, he inherited the position from his father. The manner of wearing the shield slung over the shoulders was common practice. When attacking, it could be swung to the front or to either side; in retreat, it could be suspended at the back. This method also permitted both arms the freedom to shoot the bow and arrow.

MAN OF SENSE
Iowa, 1832, oil on canvas, 29″ x 24″ (74 x 61 cm).

*Highly respected as a distinguished and brave warrior, he wears a broad silver band around
his head, bedecked with a crest of red dyed horsehair.*

SHOOTING CEDAR
Iowa, 1832, oil on canvas, 29″ x 24″ (74 x 61 cm).
This warrior wears a cloth turban headdress, acquired from the traders, and a horsehair crest.

WIFE OF BEAR-CATCHER
Kansas, 1832, oil on canvas, 29″ x 24″ (74 x 61 cm).
A sympathetic portrait, but out of drawing. Unless deformed, this woman's left arm just couldn't work the way Catlin has rendered it.

MAN OF GOOD SENSE
Kansas, 1832, oil on canvas, 29″ x 24″ (74 x 61 cm).
The Kansas were a small tribe in 1831, numbering no more than 1,560 people. They lived in earth lodges on the Kansas River, fifty miles west of its union with the Missouri.

THE WOLF
Kansas, 1832, oil on canvas, 29″ x 24″ (74 x 61 cm).
This chief wears an elaborate turban headdress, a necklace of wampum, hair pipe ear pendants, and a silver peace medal.

STRIKES TWO AT ONCE
Oto, 1832, oil on canvas, 29″ x 24″ (74 x 61 cm).
His name suggests that he earned it by striking two enemy simultaneously, no mean feat.

LOOSE PIPE-STEM
Oto, 1832, oil on canvas, 29″ x 24″ (74 x 61 cm).
For a robe, this man is wearing the complete hide of a grizzly bear, belted up with a finger-woven sash.

TAL-LEE
Osage, 1834, oil on canvas, 29″ x 24″ (74 x 61 cm).

A distinguished warrior according to Catlin —"most noted and respected." Shown here with his lance, shield, bow, and quiver, he is wearing a deer hair roach headdress. Catlin considered him a "fair specimen of the Osage figure as well as facial outline."

CLEREMONT
Osage, 1834, oil on canvas, 29" x 24" (74 x 61 cm).

First Chief of the tribe. Though a young man, he fell heir to the position upon the death of his distinguished father, with the consent of the people. The huge war club, decorated with upholstery tacks, is in the shape of a gun stock.

WA-HO-BECK-EE
Osage, 1834, oil on canvas, 29″ x 24″ (74 x 61 cm).
Said to be the handsomest of all Osages, he holds an eagle feather fan in his hand.

HE WHO TAKES AWAY, WAR, AND MINK-CHESK
Osage, 1834, oil on canvas, 29″ x 24″ (74 x 61 cm).
These three distinguished young men posed in typical summer attire: breech cloths, trade cloth robes, moccasins, beads, and roaches.

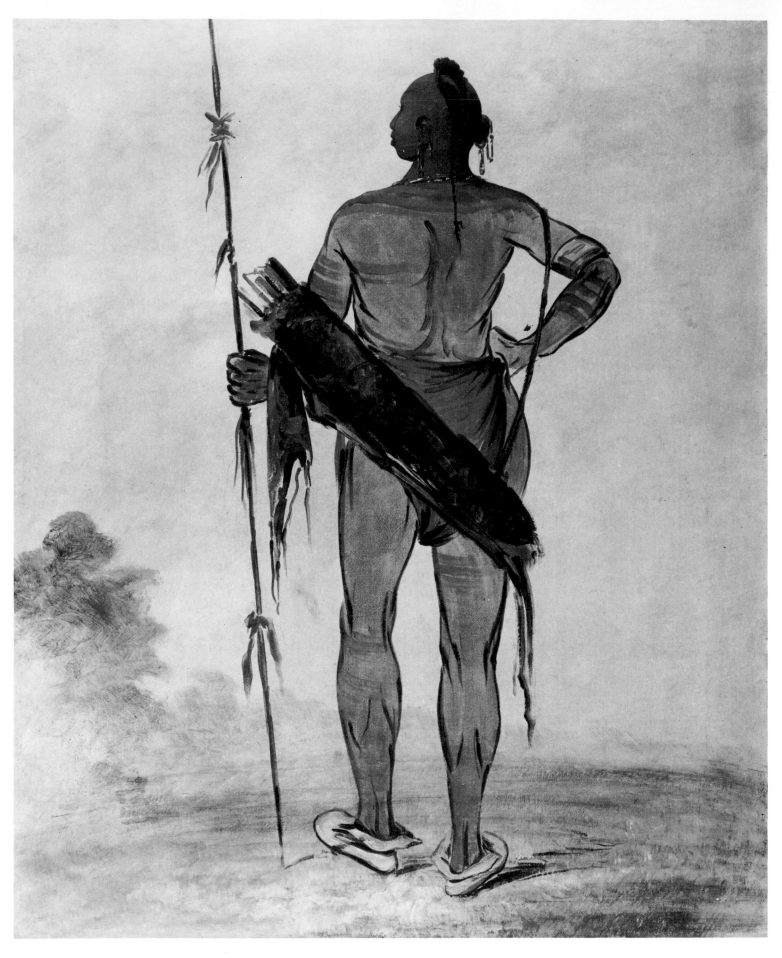

WHITE HAIR, THE YOUNGER
Osage, 1834, oil on canvas, 29″ x 24″ (74 x 61 cm).
This band chief is posed in an unusual fashion. Though the picture is sketchy, Catlin has rendered a striking portrait.

HANDSOME BIRD
Osage, 1834, oil on canvas, 29″ x 24″ (74 x 61 cm).
These spiked, ball-headed war clubs could be thrown, end-over-end, with deadly accuracy as far as fifty yards.

BUFFALO BULL
Pawnee, 1832, oil on canvas, 29″ x 24″ (74 x 61 cm).

*A member of the Grand Division, this man wears his totem painted on his chest and face.
Catlin posed many of his models perched on rocks, a sitting position Indians found most
uncomfortable. Since there were no chairs, men preferred sitting cross-legged on robes.*

THE CHEYENNE

Pawnee, 1832, oil on canvas, 29″ x 24″ (74 x 61 cm).

Typical of some of Catlin's unfinished sketches, it is, nonetheless, a powerful portrait. In his right hand, the sitter holds a quirt, in his left a catlinite pipe.

LITTLE CHIEF
Pawnee, 1832, oil on canvas, 29″ x 24″ (74 x 61 cm).
This type of headdress was popular among many of the Missouri River tribes.

BRAVE CHIEF
Pawnee, 1832, oil on canvas, 29" x 24" (74 x 61 cm).
The painted hands indicate hand-to-hand combat in which the wearer was victorious.

WOLF CHIEF
Mandan, 1832, oil on canvas, 29″ x 24″ (74 x 61 cm).

Head chief of the tribe, he was austere and overbearing, feared and respected rather than loved. In his hand, he holds two pipes, one a feathered calumet. He fell heir to his position as the eldest son of a former head chieftain.

MAH-TO-TOH-PA
Mandan, 1832, oil on canvas, 29″ x 24″ (74 x 61 cm).

Four Bears, while Second Chief of the tribe, was the most popular man in the nation. For his generosity, gentlemanliness, elegance, bravery, and good looks, Catlin considered him the most extraordinary Indian on the continent.

115

INTERIOR VIEW OF THE MANDAN MEDICINE LODGE
1832, oil on canvas, 24″ x 29″ (61 x 74 cm).

As part of the O-Kee-Pa rites, a shaman in the foreground cries to the Great Spirit as young participants look on.

BULL DANCE
Mandan, 1832, oil on canvas, 24″ x 29″ (61 x 74 cm).

As part of the O-Kee-Pa ceremony, eight men, impersonating the buffalo, danced in the plaza to assure that the herds would be plentiful. O-Kee-Ne-De, the Evil Spirit, is seen as the black painted figure to the left. He will soon be driven from the village by the powers of good and by the angered women.

RAINMAKING AMONG THE MANDANS
1837-39, oil on canvas, 19½" x 27" (50 x 69 cm).

After three other young men had failed, Hair of the White Buffalo, the young man on the roof, shot an arrow into a black cloud and the rain soon fell in torrents. Hair of the White Buffalo became a hero. Catlin noted that the Mandans never failed in their rainmaking, for one after another young man continued their incantations until rain finally came.

OLD BEAR
Mandan, 1832, oil on canvas, 29″ x 24″ (74 x 61 cm).

This shaman (or medicine man) holds two calumets, magic accoutrements of his profession.
Shamans received their curative powers through dreams and visions, through participation in
the torture ceremony of the O-Kee-Pa, and through instruction from experienced shamans.

MID-DAY SUN
Hidatsa, 1832, oil on canvas, 29″ x 24″ (74 x 61 cm).

Shown here in a white dress of mountain sheepskin decorated with dyed porcupine quills, she at first demurred to stand for her portrait, claiming that she was not pretty enough and that she would be laughed at. But her family prevailed. This painting is an example of Catlin's trouble with figures.

BUFFALO CHASE — A SURROUND BY THE HIDATSA
1832-33, oil on canvas, 24″ x 29″ (61 x 74 cm).

Catlin describes this scene as a "battle" wherein many of the hunters were either thrown from the horses and had to run for their lives or were squeezed between the rushing buffalo and escaped by running over their backs. The entire herd of several hundred buffalo were killed within fifteen minutes.

TWO CROWS
Hidatsa, 1832, oil on canvas, 29″ x 24″ (74 x 61 cm).

This chief is shown displaying his exploits on his shirt. The Hidatsa were a warlike tribe, often embroiling their neighbors, the Mandans, in their conflicts.

SIX
Plains Ojibwa, 1832, oil on canvas, 29" x 24" (74 x 61 cm).
According to Catlin. this huge chief was a man of many exploits. Some of them are recorded in pictographic form on his shirt.

SIOUX VILLAGE
1835-36, oil on canvas, 19½″ x 27⅝″ (50 x 70 cm).

This was painted at Lake Calhoun near Fort Snelling (Minnesota). In this scene of a Santee village, Catlin properly portrays the tipis in various sizes. In most of his sketches, he ignores this fact and draws them all the same size.

PIPESTONE QUARRY ON THE COTEAU DES PRAIRIES
Minnesota, 1836-37, oil on canvas, 19½" x 27¼" (50 x 69 cm).

When first mined, catlinite is soft and easily carved. Many tribes used this quarry until the Sioux preempted it in the early 19th century. Some traditions assert that the red stone was created by the blood of Indians of many nations who drowned here seeking refuge from a great flood.

BLACK ROCK
Teton Sioux, 1832, oil on canvas, 29″ x 24″ (74 x 61 cm).
*This chief of the Two Kettle Division is shown wearing a painted buffalo robe depicting his
exploits. According to Catlin, the split horn bonnet with ermine skin crown designates him to
be a war leader.*

SCALP DANCE
Teton Sioux, 1835-37, oil on canvas, 20⅛″ x 27⅜″ (51 x 69 cm).

The Sioux held victory dances after successful forays, giving the scalps to the mothers or sisters of fallen relatives who then joined in the celebration.

GREAT CHIEF
Ponca, 1832, oil on canvas, 29″ x 24″ (74 x 61 cm).

A son of Smoke, this young man, at the age of eighteen, took four wives the day before Catlin's visit, thereby raising his status immeasurably.

PIGEON'S EGG HEAD (THE LIGHT)
Assiniboine, 1837-39, oil on canvas, 29″ x 24″ (74 x 61 cm).

Catlin mistranslated this man's name which properly is "The Light." Upon his return from Washington, this once-respected man was ridiculed into ostracism by his tribesmen, who thought his tales of eastern civilization were preposterous fabrications.

THE SMOKE
Ponca, 1832, oil on canvas, 29″ x 24″ (74 x 61 cm).
This chief of the Poncas wept as he described the demise of his tribe through whiskey, smallpox, and warfare. He sadly predicted the extinction of his people, once numerous and prosperous.

PURE FOUNTAIN
Ponca, 1832, oil on canvas, 29″ x 24″ (74 x 61 cm).
Wife of Smoke, she is described by Catlin as a "young and very pretty woman." Handsomely tattooed, she is shown wearing a painted buffalo robe.

BLOODY HAND
Arikara, 1832, oil on canvas, 29" x 24" (74 x 61 cm).
*This Arikara headman is shown wearing a hair-fringed shirt pictographically decorated
with his exploits.*

THE TWIN
Arikara, 1832, oil on canvas, 29″ x 24″ (74 x 61 cm).
*Wife of Bloody Hand, she is described by Catlin as "a good looking matron." This portrait
is a particularly good example of Catlin's ability to catch the Indian character.*

ARIKARA VILLAGE OF EARTH-COVERED LODGES
1832, oil on canvas, 11¼" x 14⅜" (29 x 37 cm).
1,600 miles north of St. Louis, this village of 150 earth lodges was situated on the west bank of the Missouri River.

MINK
Mandan, 1832, oil on canvas, 29″ x 24″ (74 x 61 cm).

Catlin described her as "a beautiful girl." Her dress is decorated with both beaded and quilled medallions and with elk teeth; around her wrist, she wears a quilled bracelet.

BIRDS-EYE VIEW OF MANDAN VILLAGE
1837-39, oil on canvas, 24⅛″ x 29″ (61 x 74 cm).

A view of the central plaza. The barrel-shaped edifice in the center was called "The Big Canoe" and contained the tribe's sacred medicines. In the foreground is shown a tub-like "bull boat" perched on the roof of an earth lodge. Forty to sixty feet in diameter, the lodges might accommodate a family of twenty to forty members.

MANDAN CEMETERY
1832, oil on canvas, 11⅛″ x 14⅜″ (26 x 37 cm).

The Mandan dead were wrapped in bundles and placed on scaffolds behind the village.
When the corpses disintegrated, the bones were buried, while the skulls were placed in circles.
In the center was a mound with the skulls of a male and a female buffalo surmounted by
offering poles. Women came daily to "feed" the remains of deceased relatives.

MANDAN GAME OF TCHUNG-KEE
1832-33, oil on canvas, 19½" x 27⅝" (50 x 70 cm).

The object of the Hoop and Pole Game was to slide the long pole, to which leather tabs were attached, in such a manner as to have the rolling stone hoop fall over one of the tabs. Men would wager their possessions, sometimes gambling away everything.

MANDANS ATTACKING ARIKARAS
1832-33, oil on canvas, 19⅝″ x 27⅝″ (50 x70 cm).
Catlin only heard of this attack. According to his Letters, *the Mandans were the victors.*

MANDAN SCALPING AN ENEMY
1835-37, oil on canvas, 19⅝″ x 27⅝″ (50 x 70 cm).

Catlin makes no mention in his Letters *of having witnessed this action. However, he listened to many warriors recount such exploits, and this sketch would appear to be an accurate portrayal.*

MANDAN FOOT WAR PARTY IN COUNCIL
1832, oil on canvas, 19⅝" x 27⅝" (50 x 70 cm).

Catlin observed these men having just returned from their victory over the Arikaras. They are shown resting before entering the village.

MAH-TO-TOH-PA
Mandan, 1832, oil on canvas, 29″ x 24″ (74 x 61 cm).
Catlin's forthright portrait of Four Bears, his most respected Indian, does justice to this handsome leader.

MINT
Mandan, 1832, oil on canvas, 29″ x 23″ (74 x 58 cm).
*This twelve-year-old girl is shown with white-streaked hair, an albinism found among many
of the Mandan females. Catlin was convinced this trait was genetically inherited as the
result of admixture with Prince Madoc's lost Welsh colonists.*

RED THUNDER
Hidatsa, 1832, oil on canvas, 24″ x 24″ (61 x 61 cm).

Son of the Head Chief, Black Moccasin, he was recognized as a most desperate warrior. He is shown here in his battle attire: his bow, arrows, shield, and a bandolier containing food and medicine. Many men wore only a breech cloth and moccasins so their actions would not be hampered.

WIFE OF TWO CROWS
Hidatsa, 1832, oil on canvas, 29" x 24" (74 x 61 cm).
Catlin observed there to be "many beautiful and voluptuous women" among the Hidatsa.

WIFE OF THE SIX
Plains Ojibwa, 1832, oil on canvas, 29″ x 24″ (74 x 61 cm).
She is shown here wearing a painted buffalo robe with the hair side in, a common method for winter wear. Catlin describes her as one of Six's several wives, "though not the most agreeable."

KAY-A-GIS-GIS
Plains Ojibwa, 1832, oil on canvas, 29″ x 24″ (74 x 61 cm).

This is one of the few portraits of an Indian smiling. Too often characterized as stoical, the Indians were jovial, warm, and filled with wit when they were among close friends and relatives. This young woman is shown removing the braids from her hair and seemingly enjoying her immodesty.

TOW-EE-KA-WET
Plains Cree, 1832, oil on canvas, 29″ x 24″ (74 x 61 cm).

Tattooing was frequently more than mere decoration. More often, it was ceremonial in character and a sign of status. The stripes on this woman's chin and lower cheeks mark her as a person of rank. Catlin identifies her as the comely wife of Broken Arm.

HE WHO HAS EYES BEHIND HIM
Plains Cree, 1831, oil on canvas, 29″ x 24″ (74 x 61 cm).

Also known as "Broken Arm." It was customary among many tribes to give men several names, often as many as four. Some were given in respect for a grandparent; some were secret and often unmentionable, known only to the individual and to his parents; others were in recognition of some physical attribute or in honor of an outstanding accomplishment.

BLUE MEDICINE
Santee, 1835, oil on canvas, 29″ x 24″ (74 x 61 cm).
This shaman is shown holding his deerhide medicine or mystery drum and a sacred rattle of split deer hoofs.

BIG EAGLE
Santee, 1835, oil on canvas, 29″ x 24″ (74 x 61 cm).
*Known as "Black Dog," he was chief of the Long Avenue band. The Santee Sioux were
formerly rice gatherers in Minnesota, but were driven west by the gun-carrying Ojibwa.*

BUFFALO CHASE
1832-33, oil on canvas, 24″ x 29″ (61 x 74 cm).
The chase was extremely dangerous. Horses were often gored, and men leaped to safety if they were lucky, for the crazed buffalo were quick and determined to attack their adversaries.

BUFFALO CHASE IN WINTER

1832-33, oil on canvas, 24″ x 29″ (61 x 74 cm).

With drifts as much as three to four feet deep, the hunter on snowshoes had a real advantage over the lumbering, 2,000-pound buffalo. Catlin spent no winters on the upper Missouri, so this painting, though accurate, is from hearsay.

ONE HORN
Teton Sioux, 1832, oil on canvas, 29″ x 24″ (74 x 61 cm).
Head Chief of the Miniconjou Division, he took his name from the single shell he wore around his neck, a gift from his father. A man of many exploits, as the paintings on his shirt attest, he could run down a buffalo on foot and drive an arrow to its heart.

SAND BAR
Teton Sioux, 1832, oil on canvas, 29″ x 24″ (74 x 61 cm).

Wife of the trader, Chardon, she wears an elkskin dress profusely ornamented with brass buttons and beads. The tattooing on her chin assures her entrance in afterlife to the "Land of Many Lodges."

WAR DANCE
Teton Sioux, 1837-39, oil on canvas, 19⅜″ x 26⅝″ (49 x 68 cm).

Catlin painted several versions of war dances, performed prior to undertaking an expedition. The steps, antics, and cries mimic the ferocity of actual battle. Catlin captured the action and posturing very well.

BATTLE BETWEEN SIOUX AND SAC AND FOX
date unknown, oil on canvas, 26⅛″ x 32½″ (66 x 83 cm).

The Santee Sioux and the allied Sac and Fox were constantly at war in the 1820s and 1830s. Catlin makes no mention of this affair in his Letters; *it may be a fanciful reconstruction of a skirmish.*

SELF-TORTURE IN SIOUX CEREMONY
1835-37, oil on canvas, 19⅝" x 27¼" (50 x 69 cm).

Catlin found this Teton Sioux ceremony "curious and disgusting." More commonly practiced by several supplicants at a great tribal convocation called the Sun Dance, the object was to obtain "power" from Wakan Tanka (the Great Mystery) *through the Sun.*

THE DOG
Teton Sioux, 1832, oil on canvas, 29″ x 24″ (74 x 61 cm).
This chief of the Bad Arrow Points Band was "an ill-natured and surly man — despised by the chiefs of every other band." Shortly after this portrait was finished, he killed Little Bear of the Hunkpapa band and later was murdered by Little Bear's vengeful relatives.

TORN BELLY
Yankton Sioux, 1832, oil on canvas, 29″ x 24″ (74 x 61 cm).

A distinguished brave of the Yankton division. Among the Sioux, the locks of hair decorating the men's shirts were not scalps, but in reality, they were hair donated by the wearer's mother or sisters. Only certain leaders were entitled to wear such shirts, the locks representing the people of the tribe for whom the wearer was responsible.

RED THING THAT TOUCHES IN MARCHING
Teton Sioux, 1832, oil on canvas, 29″ x 24″ (74 x 61 cm).
This unmarried daughter of Black Rock was much esteemed by everyone for her beauty and modesty. Here she wears a painted buffalo robe of geometric design reserved for women.

DANCE OF THE CHIEFS
Teton Sioux, 1832-33, oil on canvas, 24″ x 29″ (61 x 74 cm).

*This dance was given to honor Catlin for his great "medicine" — his ability to capture the
likeness of his subjects. A shaman is drumming to the right, while four young women chant
at the left.*

TOBACCO
Teton Sioux, 1832, oil on canvas, 29″ x 24″ (74 x 61 cm).
*This Oglala chief was respected as a warrior and famous among his people. His hair-fringed
shirt is embellished with pictographs of his battles.*

BOW AND QUIVER
Comanche, 1832, oil on canvas, 29″ x 24″ (74 x 61 cm).
*Head Chief of the Comanches, he is portrayed simply attired with shell earrings, a necklace
with a pendant boar's tooth, and a headdress featuring two feathers from a golden eagle.*

MOUNTAIN OF ROCKS
Comanche, 1834, oil on canvas, 29" x 24" (74 x 61 cm).

This Second Chief of the Comanches was corpulent to the extreme, weighing over three hundred pounds, the largest and fattest Indian Catlin ever saw. Here the chief sports a thin stubble of a beard. Facial hair among Indians was sparse, and most men plucked their whiskers with shells used as tweezers.

COMANCHE VILLAGE
1834-35, oil on canvas, 19½" x 27⅝" (50 x 70 cm).
The women are shown here dressing buffalo hides as the men loll around. In the background are meat drying racks.

COMANCHE MOUNTED WAR PARTY
1834-37, oil on canvas, 19⅝" x 27⅝" (50 x 70 cm).
Catlin pictures the spirited horsemanship of the Comanches as they perform a sham battle.

WOMAN WHO STRIKES MANY
Blackfeet, 1832, oil on canvas, 29″ x 24″ (74 x 61 cm).
Shown here in a dress of mountain goatskin and the decorated robe of a young buffalo, she typically wears leggings and moccasins — the style for the well-dressed Plains Indian woman.

BUFFALO BULL'S BACK FAT
Blackfeet, 1832, oil on canvas, 29″ x 24″ (74 x 61 cm).
Head Chief of the Blackfeet, his name refers to the buffalo's hump, the most delicious part of the animal's flesh. Catlin described this fifty-year-old man as good looking and dignified.

BUFFALO CHASE WITH BOWS AND LANCES
1832-33, oil on canvas, 24" x 29" (74 x 61 cm).
In the chase with bow and lance, Catlin accurately shows the hunter's arrow penetrating the buffalo's left and preferable side — the area closest to the heart.

PRAIRIE BLUFFS
1832, oil on canvas, 11¼″ x 14½″ (29 x 37 cm).
This is one of Catlin's better landscapes — sunrise near the mouth of the Yellowstone River.

WOLF ON THE HILL (HIGH WOLF)
Cheyenne, 1832, oil on canvas, 29″ x 24″ (74 x 61 cm).
This imposing chief impressed Catlin by his height. The Cheyennes are among the tallest of all peoples, the men averaging at least six feet.

PIGEON'S EGG HEAD (THE LIGHT)
Assiniboine, 1831, oil on canvas, 29″ x 24″ (74 x 61 cm).

Son of the Chief, this man went to Washington to represent his people. The Assiniboines, known as the "Stone Boilers," separated from the Sioux as a result of two women quarreling over the division of meat.

WEE-TA-RA-SHA-RO
Wichita, 1834, oil on canvas, 29″ x 24″ (74 x 61 cm).
Head chief of the Wichita, he was ninety or more years old when this portrait was painted.

PRAIRIE MEADOWS BURNING
1832, oil on canvas, 11″ x 14⅛″ (28 x 36 cm).

Fanned by a high wind, the prairie fire was threateningly dangerous. Some were set purposely by the Indians at springtime in the belief that the grass greened earlier and became more lush feed for the horses.

DYING BUFFALO

1832-33, oil on canvas, 24″ x 29″ (61 x 74 cm).

Catlin, like many artists, had his troubles depicting the buffalo, but in this painting, he vividly portrays the death throes of a huge beast shot with an arrow in the left side, the area closest to the heart.

BUFFALO HUNT UNDER THE WOLFSKIN MASK
1832-33, oil on canvas, 24″ x 29″ (61 x 74 cm).
Disguised in wolfskins, the hunters could approach their unwary targets at close range.

WHITE WOLVES ATTACKING A BUFFALO BULL
1832?, oil on canvas, 19⅝" x 27⅝" (50 x 70 cm).
Old bulls like this one were left behind by the herds and became easy victims of the predatory wolf packs. Wolves seldom bothered the herds; rather they preyed on the very young, old, sick, or enfeebled animals.

BREAKING DOWN THE WILD HORSE
1834-35, oil on canvas, 19⅝" x 27⅝" (50 x 70 cm).

The Indian first mounted his own fastest horse and with his lariat, raced among the herd of wild horses, throwing the noose over the one of his choice. Dismounting, he kept hold of the rope and ran with his captive until the animal fell from exhaustion. After placing hobbles over its forefeet, he approached the struggling horse, placed his hand over the mustang's eyes and nose, then breathed into its nostrils.

EAGLE'S RIBS
Blackfeet, 1832, oil on canvas, 29" x 24" (74 x 61 cm).

Catlin observed that no tribe was more gaudily dressed than the Blackfeet, with the possible exception of the Crows. This member of the Piegan Division is a good example, wearing a shirt lavishly decorated with porcupine quill work.

MEDICINE MAN
Blackfeet, 1832, oil on canvas, 29″ x 24″ (74 x 61 cm).

This Blackfeet shaman wears a bearskin mask adorned with the skins of many animals, including snakes, frogs, and bats, the spirits of such animals being the source of the doctor's power to cure.

IRON HORN
Blackfeet, 1832, oil on canvas, 29" x 24" (74 x 61 cm).
This warrior wears face paint and two bald eagle feathers as badges of his "coups."

CRYSTAL STONE
Blackfeet, 1832, oil on canvas, 29″ x 24″ (74 x 61 cm).

The youngest wife of Buffalo Bull's Back Fat —of which he may have had eight —she was the "apple of his eye." This is one of many examples of Catlin's skill at catching the racial character of his subjects.

WHITE BUFFALO
Blackfeet, 1832, oil on canvas, 29″ x 24″ (74 x 61 cm).
This aged medicine man, says Catlin, "on his left arm presents his mystery drum . . . in which are concealed the hidden and secret mysteries of his healing art."

BUFFALO'S CHILD
Blackfeet, 1832, oil on canvas, 29″ x 24″ (74 x 61 cm).

This man wears a buffalo robe depicting his exploits. For striking an enemy, the Plains Indians awarded "coups" or strikes, and each "coup" was added to a man's war record. Those with the greatest number were held in the highest esteem.

INDIAN FAMILY ALARMED AT APPROACH OF A PRAIRIE FIRE
1832, oil on canvas, 20″ x 27⅜″ (51 x 69 cm).

Prairie fires traveled at the rate of the wind, sometimes up to fifty miles an hour. Alarmed at the approach of the conflagration, this family is breaking camp. Tipis could be dismantled and the belongings ready for moving within fifteen minutes.

INDIANS ON HORSEBACK ATTACKING THE GRIZZLY BEAR
1832-33, oil on canvas, 24" x 29" (61 x 74 cm).
The grizzly was considered man's most ferocious adversary, and the killing of one entitled the hunter to a "coup," as well as the right to wear a necklace of claws as a badge of bravery.

HE WHO TIES HIS HAIR BEFORE
Crow, 1832, oil on canvas, 29" x 24" (74 x 61 cm).

The Crows were noted for the length of their hair, sometimes reaching to the ground. Those unable to achieve this luxuriance often pasted on additional locks to increase the length.

CROW LODGE OF TWENTY-FIVE BUFFALO SKINS
1832-33, oil on canvas, 24" x 29" (61 x 74 cm).

*While the tipi was owned by the woman, this painted one shows the exploits of the husband.
Made by the woman, it was fashioned from the hides of twenty-five buffaloes. The shield at
the left was ceremonially turned by the owner several times a day to face the sun.*

TWO CROWS
Crow, 1832, oil on canvas, 29″ x 24″ (74 x 61 cm).

Catlin was impressed by the fine physique of the Crows and especially by their facial characteristics: "the semi-lunar outline . . . the bold and anti-angular nose with clear and rounded arch and a low and receding forehead."

RED BEAR
Crow, 1832, oil on canvas, 29" x 24" (74 x 61 cm).
Catlin's impressionistic portrait dramatically imparts the strength and character of his powerful subject.

VERY SWEET MAN
Crow, 1832, oil on canvas, 29" x 24" (74 x 61 cm).
Catlin painted his Crow subjects while they were visiting their relatives, the Hidatsa. The Crows had separated years before, giving up agriculture — save for raising tobacco — to hunt the buffalo to the west.

SHE WHO BATHES HER KNEES
Cheyenne, 1832, oil on canvas, 29″ x 24″ (74 x 61 cm).

Wife of Wolf On The Hill, her name would seem to imply that others did not bathe. On the contrary, the Indians were fastidious, often bathing daily in the streams nearby their villages and in winter even breaking the ice.

LITTLE SPANIARD
Comanche, 1834, oil on canvas, 29" x 24" (74 x 61 cm).

*Half Comanche, half Spaniard, this warrior was renowned. Ordinarily, halfbreeds were
held in contempt. To overcome this stigma, he performed the most daring deeds and won the
acclaim of the Indians.*

194

COMANCHES MOVING CAMP
1834-35, oil on canvas, 19½″ x 27⅝″ (50 x 70 cm).

Dogs, and later horses, were the Indians' beasts of burden. Dogfights often occurred. In the ensuing entanglements, the women, too, fought one another with fists as they tried to protect their property. The men, riding their horses at the side of the procession, were much amused at the predicament, but offered no help.

CARRIES A WOLF
Comanche, 1834, oil on canvas, 29″ x 24″ (74 x 61 cm).
This Comanche chief wears his shield and holds his quirt. Catlin characterized the Comanche, like the Wichita, as short and approaching corpulency, compared to the other tribes he visited.

COMANCHE FEATS OF HORSEMANSHIP
1834-35, oil on canvas, 24″ x 29″ (61 x 74 cm).

The Plains Indians were remarkable horsemen, and the Comanche were unsurpassed. These riders exhibit their skill in a sham battle, using their mounts as a shield as they shoot their arrows over the horses' backs.

THE SMOKED SHIELD
Kiowa, 1834-35, oil on canvas, 29" x 24" (74 x 61 cm).
This noted warrior was nearly seven feet tall. He was also the fastest runner in the tribe, able to run down a buffalo on foot and kill it with a knife.

THUNDERER AND WHITE WEASEL
Kiowa, 1834, oil on canvas, 29″ x 24″ (74 x 61 cm).

White Weasel enfolds her young brother in her arms. Both were captives of the Osages. The girl was returned to her people by the United States Dragoons, but her brother was killed by a charging ram the day after this portrait was finished.

TEH-TOOT-SAH (DOHASAN, LITTLE BLUFF)
Kiowa, 1834, oil on canvas, 29″ x 24″ (74 x 61 cm).

First Chief of the tribe, he is shown wearing a hair trailer of silver discs, which reached to his knees. Catlin found him to be gentlemanly and high-minded.

THIGHS
Wichita, 1834, oil on canvas, 29″ x 24″ (74 x 61 cm).
A handsome example of tattooing for which the tribe acquired its name, the Tattooed Pawnees. Catlin was much impressed by the beauty of the Wichita women.

GRASS-COVERED LODGE OF THE WICHITA
1834, oil on canvas, 24" x 19" (61 x 74 cm).

The Wichita were sedentary farmers and, as was true for all the agriculturists east of the Rockies, it was the women who tilled the fields.

BUFFALO BULLS FIGHTING IN RUNNING SEASON
1837-39, oil on canvas, 24″ x 29″ (61 x 74 cm).

Catlin used the early Plainsmen's term "running season" for "rutting season." Here the bulls challenged one another for dominance. Vanquished leaders often left the herds to wander alone.

BIBLIOGRAPHY

Catlin, George. *Letters and Notes on the Manners, Customs and Conditions of the North American Indians*. 2 vols. London: 1841.

——— *O-Kee-Pa, A Religious Ceremony and other Customs of the Mandans*. Edited by John C. Ewers. New Haven: Yale University Press, 1967

——— *North American Indian Portfolio*. Introduction by Harold McCracken. Chicago: Sage Books, 1970.

Ewers, John C., et al. *Early White Influence Upon Plains Indian Painting*. Seattle: Shorey, 1957.

Haberly, Lloyd. *Pursuit of the Horizon*. New York: Macmillan, 1948.

Haverstock, Mary S. *Indian Gallery: The Story of George Catlin*. New York: School Book Services, 1973.

McCracken, Harold. *George Catlin and the Old Frontier*. New York: Dial Press, 1959.

Plate, Robert. *Palette and Tomahawk*. New York: David McKay, 1962.

Rockwell, Anne. *Paintbrush and Peacepipe*. New York: Atheneum, 1971.

Roehm, Marjorie C., ed. *The Letters of George Catlin & His Family: A Chronicle of the American West*. Berkeley: University of California Press, 1966.

INDEX